CAPITALIST CRUSADER

'In clear, accessible and compelling language, Herman Mashaba explains why South Africans should embrace true capitalism and reverse the erosion of democratic values and economic freedom. His arguments, supported by facts and figures, leave no room for doubt that South Africans face a simple choice: ignore him and endure economic stagnation and social conflict, or embrace his message and enjoy what the defeat of apartheid made possible. He exposes one of the country's great tragedies, the extent to which self-serving politicians and officials are preventing the liberation, emancipation and empowerment of black South Africans.'

Leon Louw, Executive Director, Free Market Foundation

'I first met Herman around 1989, after my then-boss at African Bank, the visionary Mr Gaby Magomola, asked us Young Turks at the bank to target black entrepreneurs as a bedrock of the newly established corporate banking division within the bank. I met Mr Mashaba at his Mabopane factory where he took me and my colleagues on a tour around the facility. This was at a time when apartheid was still the official policy of the country, with its abominable and stifling impact on black lives. Yet here was this man, striding confidently as he showed us around. Obviously young, gifted and … yes, black like me *nogal*! I repeat … Black Like Me! I remember going back to my homeboys in Soweto that evening, filled with pride for this black entrepreneur and a sense that, despite the horrors of apartheid, we could all rise and be captains of our own fate. I am glad to say all four of those friends who received my animated report, including myself, have been independent job-creating entrepreneurs pretty much since then! By being an entrepreneur and a role model, Herman encouraged not only my group but many others, I am sure, through the length and breadth of this country. Love him or hate him, agree with him or not, there are three things I can always say about Herman without any fear of contradiction: First, the man is an epitome of successful black enterprise. Second, the man speaks from the heart and speaks fearlessly, and most importantly … third, this man is a patriot! They don't come more patriotic than Mr Mashaba. Instead of sitting quietly in his corner and enjoying the fruits of his hard-earned success, he comes out fighting in this book. Fighting for us to be a winning nation! Read this book and be riveted. Be ready to be challenged. Be ready to be knocked out of your comfort zone. But more importantly, be ready to be inspired like me and my crew were 26 years ago!'

Phinda M Madi, Professor Emeritus, Rhodes University

'Herman Mashaba has established significant credibility as a single-minded and successful entrepreneur. This hard-hitting book makes a significant contribution to the discussion about South Africa's future. I hope many take the time to read this penetrating analysis and think through its conclusions and implications, and respond to the call for action.'

Nicholas Binedell, Professor, Gordon Institute of Business Science

'I was delighted when Herman Mashaba, whom I have known and revered for his strong and somewhat radical views on the development of the South African economy, informed me he had written a book. Mashaba, as a successful entrepreneur and industrialist, is also a vigorous proponent of the free enterprise system, based on his experience.

His divergent views and contentions on the current government policies in South Africa, elaborately dealt with in this book, deserve to be given considerable attention in light of the fact that the country presently requires appropriate policies that will enable it to conquer the increasing problems of poverty, unemployment and slow economic growth. Mashaba's book has come at the right moment in our history.'

Dr Samuel Mokgethi Motsuenyane

CAPITALIST CRUSADER

FIGHTING POVERTY THROUGH ECONOMIC GROWTH

HERMAN MASHABA

ISBN: 978-1-928257-05-9

e-ISBN: 978-1-928257-06-6

First edition, first impression 2015

Published by Bookstorm (Pty) Ltd

PO Box 4532

Northcliff 2115

Johannesburg

South Africa

www.bookstorm.co.za

Distributed by On the Dot

www.onthedot.co.za

Edited by Sally Antrobus

Proofread by Sean Fraser

Cover design by mr design

Cover image courtesy of 21 Icons South Africa:
www.21icons.com

Cover image by Gary van Wyk

Book design and typesetting by Triple M

Printed by ABC Press, Cape Town

CONTENTS

ABBREVIATIONS

AMCU	Association of Mineworkers and Construction Union
ANC	African National Congress
ANCYL	ANC Youth League
ASGISA	Accelerated and Shared Growth Initiative South Africa
BBBEE	broad-based black economic empowerment
BEE	black economic empowerment
CCMA	Commission for Conciliation, Mediation and Arbitration
CEO	chief executive officer
COPE	Congress of the People
COSATU	Congress of South African Trade Unions
DA	Democratic Alliance
DP	Democratic Party
EFF	Economic Freedom Fighters
FMF	Free Market Foundation

GDP	gross domestic product
GEAR	Growth, Employment and Redistribution
HR	human resource/human resources
ILO	International Labour Organisation
IMF	International Monetary Fund
MD	managing director
NDP	National Development Plan
NGO	non-governmental organisation
NGP	New Growth Path
NPA	National Prosecuting Authority
NUM	National Union of Mineworkers
OECD	Organisation for Economic Co-operation and Development
PIC	Public Investment Company
RDO	rock drill operator
RDP	Reconstruction and Development Programme
SACP	South African Communist Party
SACTWU	Southern African Clothing and Textile Workers' Union
SANCO	South African National Civic Organisation
SMEs	small and medium enterprises
StatsSA	Statistics South Africa
UDF	United Democratic Front

FOREWORD

by Yuri N Maltsev

I strongly recommend Herman Mashaba's new book, *Capitalist Crusader*, to everyone interested in the past, present and future of our beloved South Africa. Based on impeccable economic and statistical research and historical analysis, it is a brilliantly written blueprint for freedom and prosperity for the people of South Africa. It is also a personal message of a deeply concerned South African based on his outstanding personal experience as a citizen, entrepreneur and educator. It is a momentous contribution to the ongoing search for solutions for the most important economic and social problems of South Africa.

In *Capitalist Crusader* Herman provides a synthesis of deeply personal experiences, his own and those of others, with vast and solid academic research, to present his decisive case for renewal of South African democracy on the basis of Mandela's legacy of political and economic freedom. Herman is uniquely qualified to be a crusader for capitalism: he was born into the socialist slavery of apartheid and was deprived of both economic and political freedom. As a world-renowned entrepreneur, much-heralded civic leader, prolific writer, popular and compelling public speaker and dedicated educator, he has come a long way from the naïve, anti-capitalist and anti-white rhetoric of his teenage days in Ga Ramotse near Hammanskraal, when he had holes in his shoes and anger in his heart. I have had the privilege to attend Herman's presentations to various audiences in South Africa and the United States and I can attest to his superb communication skills. His humour is irresistibly contagious. His management methods are studied all over the world and quoted in the most popular textbooks on management in the West[1] and East.

Mashaba's book *Black Like You* is a captivating personal story of a man who struggled for his economic and human freedom and won against all odds and obstacles imposed on him by the inhuman system of apartheid. His memoir reflects Mashaba's optimistic character, his almost nuclear energy and great personal charm. This synergy has produced a fascinating result: a great life full of struggle, setbacks and success, personal achievement so generously shared with others, hope projected on millions of South Africans fighting for their survival against the bureaucratic state machinery tilted against them today.

Speaking about *Capitalist Crusader*, Herman told me: 'My real motivation behind the book is to encourage South Africans to take responsibility for the future of the country. We can't afford to sit back and watch politicians do as they please, and only complain behind their backs. That is why nations fail.'

And I understand that very well because I come from a failed nation myself. My homeland, the Union of Soviet Socialist Republics, was spread over 11 time zones and covered a sixth of the Earth's surface. Like South Africa, it was endowed with rich natural resources, ethnic and cultural diversity, and people eager to embrace change and improve their lives and the lives of their children. They were the first in the world to embrace socialism and they were the first to face its harvest of sorrow. Their hopes and aspirations were frustrated by the intrusive and coercive government fighting the very human nature of mutual exchange and market cooperation. In its quest for 'equality', tens of millions were murdered and starved to death in a dreadful Gulag. Coercion and mass murder were the inevitable outcome of fighting free markets, free speech, free minds ... The great Russian writer and political prisoner Vasily Grossman wrote over 50 years ago: 'I used to think freedom was freedom of speech, freedom of the press, freedom of conscience. But freedom is the whole life of everyone. Here is what it amounts to: you have to have the right to sow what you wish to, to make shoes or coats, to bake into bread the flour ground from the grain you have sown, and to sell it or not sell it as you wish; for the lathe operator, the steelworker, and the artist it's a matter of being able to live as you wish and work as you wish and not as they order you to. And in our country there is no freedom—not for those who write books, nor for those who sow grain nor for those who make shoes.'[2]

This notion of the wholeness of human freedom—economic, cultural and political—is the major theme of *Capitalist Crusader*. Mashaba dissects South African economic, social and political problems and reveals their interdependence. In so doing, he provides a very attractive alternative to the economic and social crisis that we face today: a free society based on constitutional liberties, the rule of law, property rights and other human rights, freedom of exchange, and freedom of association. And it is this agenda that will unite rather than divide South Africans, no matter what their background, race, ethnicity or social position.

After the fall of socialism in the Soviet Union and Eastern and Central Europe, and certainly after the wide-ranging demolition of another form of socialism—the racialist–socialist system of apartheid in South Africa—who can possibly defend socialism today? Can we learn a lesson from this miserable failure?

It looks like the only lesson of history is that it teaches us nothing. We see a revival of socialist menace coupled with racism and politics of division. Many South Africans, smart otherwise, but brainwashed by power-hungry ANC politicians and the educational system that they created to keep the 'masses in check', still blame apartheid and colonialism for their poverty and deprivation. Our mutual friend, eminent African-American economist Walter Williams, concluded in *South Africa's War against Capitalism*: 'The whole ugly history of apartheid has been an attack on free markets and the rights of individuals, and a glorification of centralised government power ... South Africa's apartheid is not the corollary of free-market or capitalist forces. Apartheid is the result of anti-capitalistic or socialistic efforts to subvert the operation of market (capitalistic) forces.'

Socialists of all kinds have long attempted to present the South African apartheid system as some kind of right-wing capitalist abuse, an extreme form of capitalist exploitation. Nothing could be further from the truth! Ruthless racial discrimination against black South Africans in the labour market was initiated by white labour unions beginning in the 1920s. These unions were associated with various socialist movements in Soviet Russia as well as in Britain and the United States. The Communist Party of South Africa supported the white miners in their call to preserve racist wages and the colour bar with the slogan, 'Workers of the world, unite and fight for a white South Africa!'[3] This approach was later institutionalised by the government of the National Party. It was a pervasive system of government manipulation, regulation, regimentation and control. Mashaba shows that it is the exact opposite to free-market capitalism based on individual liberty and the rule of law.

As a result of a widespread anti-capitalist mentality in today's South Africa, capitalism remains a much-maligned concept as the ANC politicians, educational system and mass media that they control persuade disadvantaged South Africans to consider capitalism to be twinned with apartheid and have the notion that capitalism was one of apartheid's weapons for impoverishing the black majority. Jacob Zuma, Jessie Duarte, Rob Davis and other elements within the ANC supported this fallacy to avoid their own responsibility for a sorry state of the economy and social services. They boost their own power through restrictive legislature and regulations and pit South Africans against each other on the basis of income, skin pigmentation and ethnic origin. They are trying to create a power base of angry and poor people who would give them their votes and support for promises of handouts and massive income redistribution from productive members of society.

The irony of history is that the ongoing attack on free markets and personal freedom is conducted in today's South Africa by many of those who suffered and fought against apartheid but were later corrupted by almost unlimited power and cronyism. The ANC has abandoned its legacy of struggle for freedom and prosperity and is the major obstacle towards achieving these goals. 'In reality the DA, not the ANC, has become the party of Mandela's dream of a rainbow nation,' notes Mashaba.

In order to break the ANC's stranglehold on society and the economy and free South Africans from this party's economic plantation, Herman explores rampant corruption and mismanagement of the ANC leadership. Armed with solid economic research, he demonstrates that the ANC's policies of socialism and dependency on government handouts pave the pathway to mass poverty and are fiscally unsustainable ...

Poverty is not a cause but a result of South Africa's political problems. Like everyone else, South Africans 'need personal liberty'. 'That,' writes Walter Williams, 'means a political system in which there are guarantees of private property rights, free markets, honest government and the rule of law. Africa's poverty is, for the most part, self-inflicted.'[4]

The best way of teaching is to tell stories and this book is full of them—compelling and dramatic stories of struggle and success, of Herman and other outstanding South Africans. These stories validate an impressive amount of research and statistical data and serve as gateways to our understanding of the labour market imperfections and rigidity imposed by the over-regulation by COSATU and its minions at the Department of Labour, as well as of government micro- and macro-economic policies impeding economic growth, creating mass unemployment, destroying the human capital of the nation through a substandard educational system, and causing a mass brain drain of educated and skilled labour. The volume is an outstanding economic treatise and contributes a lot to the current scientific literature on South Africa, as well as to the ongoing socialism/capitalism controversy worldwide.

Capitalist Crusader is the antidote to the spread of anti-capitalist mentality; it exposes the dangerous system of socialist thought and presents a clear alternative to socialist slavery—a free society based on free markets and personal freedom.

The book also has a very important international significance: South African problems are not unique and, to a certain degree, very similar problems are present in most Western countries and the developing world alike. The ability to deal with and overcome these problems requires both outstanding leaders and active citizens, who 'must be open and tolerant'; must respect justice, the rule of law, and democracy; and must be willing to defend perspectives and listen to and stand up for others.

Mashaba insists: 'No subgroup of South Africans is superior to another. We are equal. We are all entitled to live in a prosperous country, where we can work at jobs of our choice earning wages of our own determination, where we can send our children to school confident that they are receiving a sound education, where we can go jogging in the neighbourhoods without carrying a can of mace or taking a guard dog along—and where investors are willing to invest because they're confident that their assets are protected by the law.' This is surely possible if the people of South Africa fully understand and embrace his message and unite to demand the future that majority rule promises. A future based on the solid foundation of human rights, the rule of law, and economic and political freedom. South Africa has all the ingredients for success, but what has been missing is a clear understanding by the majority of South Africans that only freedom can lead to prosperity. Herman Mashaba and his associates at the Free Market Foundation and Democratic Alliance are trying to reverse negative trends before it is too late and return to Mandela's vision of a free and prosperous 'rainbow nation'—a shining example of social harmony and human dignity for Africa and the world.

Yuri N Maltsev, Professor of Economics, Carthage College
Fairmont Hot Springs, British Columbia, July 2015

INTRODUCTION

South Africa's economic trajectory is very obviously off course. We are facing a serious crisis of poverty, unemployment, and inequality. I believe I have a fair understanding of the difficulties encountered by young black people because I have been there too, and I want to suggest some solutions to facilitate positive change in South Africa's fortunes.

When I co-founded the hair care business and factory Black Like Me in 1985, we lived in the sorry world of apartheid. We were searching for ways out of extremely difficult circumstances. When Nelson Mandela became South Africa's president in 1994, I thought my struggle for personal and economic freedom was over. But instead, more than 20 years later, those of us in the commercial and manufacturing sectors see our freedoms being eroded through restrictive economic controls.

I believe we can free South Africans from poverty through a firm commitment to capitalist principles. My purpose in this book is to outline the ways to escape entrenched un-employment. *Capitalist Crusader* is intended to show how each of us can contribute to eradicating poverty and consolidating our political freedom by working hard for our own economic freedom.

Herman Mashaba
July 2015

CHAPTER I

POLICY STILL HOLDS US BACK

Apartheid was a monstrous imposition, and as a start we should recognise the wide-ranging harm it did. Yet we also need to acknowledge that other kinds of policies can deliver their own varieties of harm. The National Party came to power in South Africa in 1948, and over the next four decades they enforced one Act after another that institutionalised their policy of apartheid and completely dehumanised and enslaved the black population. The following review of the National Party's successive racist policies traces how apartheid caused untold misery to the black population.

The Population Registration Act of 1950 was the foundation upon which apartheid was constructed, namely the racial classification of the population. This single act would determine the life I was legally entitled to as a black person. It classified black people as less than—less than whites, less capable of intellectual thought, less capable of living decently, less inclined to a thorough education, less entitled to work of their choice—and it barred the black population from a human quality of life. Essentially, before I was born, the government had limited my opportunities as a black child.

I was born in 1959 in the backwater of Hammanskraal, in the very year during which Prime Minister Dr HF Verwoerd, the architect of apartheid, pushed through the Promotion of Bantu Self-government Act. It ramped up his party's campaign to entrench rigid segregation legally by abolishing representation for black people and relegating the entire black South African population to homelands. There we were expected to develop our own political and cultural institutions—homelands being situated in non-urban areas that were isolated from commercial hubs.

However, prior to my birth, laws had already been passed that would determine the path my life could take. The Group Areas Act of 1950 confined all racial groups to their own residential and commercial areas. This Act forced thousands of non-whites out of their homes and businesses into areas that held no cultural or economic significance for them. No cognisance was taken of a black person's right to live where it was convenient, or to work or run a business where it was financially viable. The Group Areas Act devastated the personal lives and livelihoods of hundreds of thousands of people. It was apartheid's precedent of enslavement of the black population. A black person enjoyed absolutely no rights of citizenship—my father could not buy or rent a home near the pharmacy in central Johannesburg where he worked, and my mother could not live near us because we were economically isolated in Hammanskraal, and she could only find domestic work in Johannesburg. Black miners were accommodated in hostels near the mines purely because they had to keep the labour wheels of the mines turning, and domestic workers were tolerated in rooms in the back yards of white homes to raise white children while their mothers and fathers could work close to home and provide their children with lifestyles we black children never even dreamed of.

The Bantu Laws Amendment Act of 1952 placed severe limitations on black people who had the right to reside permanently in urban areas, and forcibly removed from urban areas anyone who did not meet these criteria. Apartheid policies such as these ensured that we were allowed to participate in the economy and reside in the urban areas only in so far as our participation would boost the South African economy.

These racist laws of separateness resulted in families being divided, and each of the successive laws that the government enacted further embedded separateness on every level: the racial divide, economic separation, and social disconnection. From the age of two, I was raised in Hammanskraal by my older sisters, our family having been successfully and irrevocably divided by apartheid's evil policies.

The oddly named Abolition of Passes Act of 1952 had done away with the 'pass' that we were expected to carry, but it substituted the pass with a far more controlling national document that detailed the holder's entire personal and job history, fingerprints, and rights of movement within the country. Every black

3

person from the age of 16 was compelled to carry this reference book, and failure to do so meant arrest and appearing in front of the Bantu Commissioner. From 1956, anyone who was apprehended without a reference book was arrested and sentenced and was not allowed to appeal the sentence imposed by the Bantu Commissioner's Court. The powers of this severely controlling Act were later extended, allowing police to raid dwellings to drive out undesirables. I recall being woken up several times as a child by policemen flashing their torchlight into our eyes, shouting and knocking over our personal possessions, demanding that we point out the hiding place of any person they thought we might be harbouring. These home invasions were extreme and humiliating incidents of harassment, and they were terrifying to me as a young child, since the only protection I had was from my older sisters, who were no match against the brutality of the police force. Hammanskraal residents were particularly vulnerable to this invasive onslaught because we lived close to a police training college and were considered fair game for the recruits to practise their skills of intimidation and terror. I still possess a copy of the brown reference book that I often show my children to remind them about the past. I had to apply for that reference book before I actually turned 16 because of my regular travel to Johannesburg to visit my mother. My school regularly had to sign that I was still a student.

The Bantu Education Act, passed in 1953, meant that the type of education I would receive was likewise determined before I was born. Black education fell under state control and was intentionally designed to reduce the quality of education black children received. It aligned such substandard education with what the government deemed our inferior black minds were capable of—menial and unskilled labour. This was yet another law intended to fracture the morale of black people and to enslave us to a white economic ruling class. Law after law was enacted to strengthen the National Party's power base and cement racially exclusive policies. In essence, basic human freedoms were continually denied to black people through damning apartheid legislation.

Further maintaining the whiteness of urban areas, the Reservation of Separate Amenities Act was passed in 1953, ensuring separate amenities for different races, and the dastardly demeaning 'whites only' and 'non-whites only' signs were erected. These meant that my mother could take her young white charges to play in the local park, but she could not sit on a 'whites only' park bench to observe them. She could go to the butcher to buy meat for her madam, but she had to use the 'non-whites only' entrance to do so. My father could assist in the sorting and shelving of medicines at the back of the pharmacy, but he could not step up to the counter and serve white customers. These laws enshrining what came to be known as 'petty apartheid' were an ignoble separation of races, and they were so acutely entrenched that many, many years later, when my wife Connie and I stepped onto a Durban beach for the first time, we were aware that even though the law had been repealed, we were stepping where our entire black nation had been refused access for almost 40 years.

Apartheid policies were the finely tuned armour that the National Party machine used to dehumanise black people at every turn. One of the most foul laws was the Suppression of Communism Act of 1950, which was used extensively to silence anyone deemed to be a critic of the apartheid regime and racial segregation. The Act defined communism as any scheme aimed to render political, industrial, social, or economic change within the country, and it enabled the government to gag anyone deemed to be a critic of government policies, to silence anyone who advocated for civil rights, and to punish people without trial. The government defended apartheid on the basis that it sought to protect South Africa against the so-called communists. In reality the government indoctrinated the white minority so that they didn't really see any difference between the *rooi gevaar* (communism) and the *swart gevaar* (black people), who, according to the National Party government, were both equally dangerous to national security. The Cold War between the West and the Soviet Union further complicated South Africa's situation, and the South African government was able to convince the West to help defend the country against the communist onslaught, and by association the false danger of the black people. This particular Act meant that, by default, as a black child I was a communist, a danger, and justifiably relegated to third-class citizenship and a life of being enslaved and controlled.

I often ask myself whether the National Party had any idea of the devastating long-term effects that the apartheid legislation would have on the enduring psyche of millions of South Africans, their social disintegration, and the economic hardship that they would endure. The aim of apartheid policy was to divide the nation racially on the basis of colour and to exclude the black majority from any form of participation in the country's politics, enslaving them only as suited their purposes. These laws and policies definitely decimated the foundations of black society and devastated both black morale and economic power, limiting us at every turn, so that we had no option but to endure the miserable conditions foisted upon us.

Living in Hammanskraal under this apartheid regime most certainly shaped my life. Apartheid policies determined my family's dire living conditions and, to a large degree, our strategies for coping with such difficult circumstances. Without the day-to-day guidance and support of our forcibly absent parents, my sisters and I had to forge our own way in the world, and very often our strategies were constructed in reaction to our situation and environment. Like most other homelands and townships, Hammanskraal did not have access to basic amenities—water and electricity. If we needed water, we stole it from the nearby farm; we simply didn't have money to pay for it. What else were we to do to supply life's most basic need? If we required warmth or fuel for cooking, we stole the wood from another nearby farm. This theft was not occasioned by greed but by pure necessity.

Under such adverse circumstances, it is easy to see why so

many black people resort to a lifelong pattern of theft. When you don't have access to basic commodities, what other options do you have? After she was widowed and became the sole breadwinner, my mother's R29-a-month salary was grossly insufficient to provide for five children, so who could blame her for stealing some sugar or flour from her employer to keep the wolf from her children's door? Theft was such a regular topic of discussion at social events that it seemed like a natural means of survival. Stealing from white people was actually celebrated and encouraged. The irony of it was that despite our weekly thieving raids, we all went to church every Sunday. Growing up in Hammanskraal during the 1960s and '70s was difficult and sometimes full of hopelessness, and I have documented those daily trials in my autobiography, *Black Like You*, released in 2012.

During my youth I was extremely resistant to interaction with white people, believing them to be the architects of suppression and responsible for the undignified way in which many black people were forced to survive. Having listened to accounts by family and friends of their encounters with white people, I could not entertain the notion of going to work in a white family's garden for a slice of bread, a cup of tea, and a couple of rand. In my mind, white people were evil creatures.

It was my dream to become a political scientist, and my sister Esther and my brother-in-law Nkokoto Parkies were determined to help me achieve my goal. They made every sacrifice to ensure my university fees were paid at the University of the North. In 1980 the university was temporarily closed due to the political unrest of the time. As students we were protesting and demanding the release of fellow students, and as a result of tension between the university administration and students, classes were boycotted for about two weeks. Instead of addressing the students' grievances, the university administration opted for military intervention. That was typical of the apartheid system in operation.

When the university reopened after a month, I decided not to return and abandoned my education. I was an angry young man who wanted to help bring about a change in the government, and I was prepared to do whatever I had to do. I desperately wanted to leave the country and join Umkhonto we Sizwe, the armed branch of the struggle machinery. I wanted the Russians to give me an AK-47 and train me to use the rifle so that I could return to kill all the white people whom I regarded as evil. At the same time, I was angry, and disappointed in the West, in particular UK Prime Minister Margaret Thatcher and US President Ronald Reagan. These two world leaders represented the democratic system that I admired, but I could not reconcile myself with the rationale behind their openly defending the apartheid system that the world regarded as a crime against humanity. They resisted any resolutions by the United Nations to impose sanctions against South Africa. The liberation movements and leaders, including Nelson Mandela, were labelled as terrorists. Fortunately, the collapse of the Soviet Union in 1989 helped facilitate the collapse of the apartheid regime as well. My attempts to join Umkhonto we Sizwe were unsuccessful, and after a severe bout of depression and questioning my future and myself, I began to grasp that I needed a change in mindset.

I soon realised that if I wanted to become economically active, then I would have to reconsider my attitude towards white people, with whom I'd attempted to avoid contact for so long. If I wanted to be a productive member of society, I had to find work, and the only people who could offer me a job were whites. So I took a job at Spar in Pretoria, where I was employed as a dispatch clerk because I was fortunate to be one of the few applicants who could read and write. The effects of National Party policy of confining black labour to menial jobs only were clearly evident. The Bantu education system was a dismally inferior product, and even among the few students who managed to make it through high school, often their literacy and numeracy levels were weak.

My experience at Spar confirmed that there were indeed racist whites; however, and more importantly, it also confirmed that if I worked hard, I could engineer my own future. Within two-and-a-half years I had elevated myself from a dispatch clerk to starting my own business. There are most certainly cases of white people exploiting black workers, but the white companies did not exploit me; indeed, it was I who used them to elevate myself from the bottom rung of the employment ladder, working my way through my goals until I was able to start a business, which I believed, and later proved, was the road to personal freedom.

I started my business Black Like Me in 1985 during the height of apartheid. The entire system was stacked against a black person getting a decent job, and we were even less likely to start our own businesses. In those days only Afrikaners had job protection. At that time they enjoyed the benefit of a quota system ensuring that jobs would go to them because of the colour of their skin, and they could take advantage of having a civil servant relative who could secure them work with benefits in the local municipality. The restrictions on black people were in full force and effect in 1985 when I started out in the hair care business, but instead of kowtowing to the law and being content with being employed, I did the unthinkable. I took on a white partner, accepted a loan, and obediently opened my business in Bophuthatswana, the black homeland in which I'd grown up, adhering to the exclusive business laws of the time—exclusive in the sense that the economy was geared to the establishment of white-owned businesses.

I decided to make the system work for me. I needed the expertise of a chemist and initially thought I could employ a black man who had worked in the industry. It soon became apparent that he did not have the chemical and management skills required, and when I had to consider employing someone else, the only respected beauty industry chemist I knew who was capable of the job and who might consider throwing in his lot with me was a white man and an Afrikaner—Johan Kriel. Such an arrangement was unheard of in 1985.

By the time democracy was established in South Africa in

1994, I was already a successful capitalist. It was entirely unnecessary for me to seek out the black economic empowerment (BEE) appointments that were elevating black business people. I had sufficient money to ensure comfort for my family, and I had the business to rebuild and run after the devastating fire just before the dawn of our democracy. When Parliament started debating bringing legislation to enact black economic empowerment, I realised that with or without me, BEE was going to be a reality in the country's economic landscape. We all thought the process would be short-lived and smooth. At about the same time, my white business colleagues were knocking at my door daily asking that I invest in their businesses. This resulted in the establishment of my investment company in 2002 to focus on such opportunities. I was able to hand over the reins of Black Like Me in 2004 to my wife. During the first 10 years of our democracy I supported the African National Congress. It was encouraging to see that housing, electrification, and provision of water were priorities for the government and that jobs previously the preserve of white people were now being taken up by qualified black applicants. But gradually I began to have doubts about the focus of the ANC. It seemed as though the ANC itself was the main priority, that party leadership instead of national leadership seemed to have taken over, and that personal agendas instead of national priorities were prevalent.

Various incidents began triggering alarm bells for me, such as Thabo Mbeki's open support (quiet diplomacy) for land grabbing by the Zimbabwe African National Union–Patriotic Front, resulting in Zimbabweans suffering massive human rights violations; the emergence in South Africa of crony capitalism by cadres close to power; corruption in the civil service happening almost with impunity; and failure to provide appropriate education to poor people. South African blacks and some whites had fought for freedom, and yet instead of our leaders supporting and imposing laws that would elevate the humanity in the country and on the continent, their policies soon began to resemble the policies of our oppressors of old.

By 2004 the situation had degenerated to such an extent that I decided that I could no longer support the ANC and I cast my first vote for the Democratic Alliance. As the 2014 election approached, I knew I could no longer maintain a tacit approval of the government and its abhorrent policies while voting for the DA. I had no faith in the ANC whatsoever, especially in light of the president's inability to prioritise the most urgent needs of the nation, namely poverty and employment. Institutions of democracy were being eroded, the free press mandated by our Constitution was being challenged and limited, and divisiveness began to show. I was hopeful that the electorate would send the government a message of dissatisfaction, but I decided that if the ANC won more than 60% of the vote, I would have to announce my commitment to challenging them and help in facilitating the creation of a viable and credible opposition that represented the aspirations of all South Africans.

While I have always kept myself informed of political events, business has been my main focus. However, as the 2014 election drew nearer, and I feared that the ANC would in fact have a good election result, I realised it was time to consider how I could contribute to the political future of the country. I paid attention to political conversations taking place across the country among my friends, colleagues, and associates. Participation as an interested observer and listener was no longer an option, and I decided I would publicly join the Democratic Alliance in order to play an active role in trying to achieve the South Africa that I believe all reasonable South Africans really want.

I am not a politician; I am foremost an entrepreneur. I believe in capitalism as a way of life, a natural system that is an enabler of economic prosperity, a supporter of freedom, and a natural means of allowing every single citizen to be an economic participant. In this book, I draw from my own experiences and education, both national and international, to illustrate how I envisage a South Africa engineered by the democratic principles that were enshrined in the Constitution drawn up after 1994 and propelled by capitalism.

Capitalism is a much-maligned concept in South Africa among those who have never overcome their prejudicial connection of capitalism and apartheid. Many previously and currently disadvantaged South Africans consider capitalism to be twinned with apartheid and have the notion that capitalism was one of apartheid's weapons for impoverishing the black majority. Communist elements within the country supported this fallacy to boost their own restrictive policies. Apartheid's economic system was racially based, and whites could flourish under capitalism, but success was essentially denied to the black population. If Bantu education had been up to the standard of white education, and capitalism had been allowed to take root and develop in black areas, black people would have been far better off. The whole country would have been richer socially and economically. The informal traders would have been able to establish their own businesses legally and would have had the necessary education to take their enterprises into business centres, employ staff, and train new workers. It was not capitalism that restrained economic growth for black people; it was the evil alliance of Bantu education and black disempowerment that kept people from being self-sufficient and entrepreneurial. Entrepreneurship is a natural way out of poverty. When desperate people need to feed their families, they turn to their own skills and use these to earn money.

There are as many staunch opponents of capitalism as there are proponents. I am one of the latter who believes that capitalism, as a natural system, has stood its ground for half a millennium. The other two major economic systems, socialism and communism, developed at around the same time, but they are very different. Capitalism is an economic system that encourages private ownership, the investment of capital, and manufacturing and distribution of commodities, with prices determined by the free market instead of the state. Profit seeking motivates any capitalist venture. Socialism refers to state ownership of common property and the means of production.

Communism refers to communal ownership of property and uses economic equality to achieve social equality. Communism promotes the notions that all labour belongs to the individual and that profit belongs partly to the labourer, not only to the business owner. It is considered exploitation if the labourer does not share in the profit.

Most countries usually combine elements of more than one system. Capitalism refers strictly to economic systems, while communism and socialism refer to both government and economic systems. To clarify, South Africa is currently a socio-capitalist country, socialist in the sense that we have public schools and spaces, social benefits, and utilities, and capitalist in that we embrace free markets. At present it would appear that through legislation, South Africa is trying to fashion a new model. There is a faction in the ANC-led government that would have us believe capitalism is evil. If this is indeed the case, then what do they suggest? How else can South Africa operate in a world that works on an international monetary system? What alternative system will work in isolation from the rest of the world? Possibly it can happen in some mythical country where oil allows government to give citizens money for nothing, as modelled in tiny Qatar, but generally it's impossible for an economy to exist in isolation from the rest of the world. The exceptions of North Korea and Cuba are hanging on to the shaky strands of communism (though they incorporate capitalist aspects when it suits them), but they are able to do so only because dissent is not tolerated in those countries.

As an entrepreneur and a capitalist, my immediate concern is how current government policies are eroding entrepreneurship and contributing to the critical shortage of jobs. There are undoubtedly numerous factors that need to be considered to create the appropriate environment for employment to take place, namely political stability, the rule of law, opportunity creation, fundamental infrastructure, good communication networks, etc. South Africa has many of these structures in viable form, some created during apartheid and some created by the ANC. Instead of being hung up on the who and why, let's capitalise on the infrastructure and sustainable structures that we do have. For example, South Africa's pre-democracy railway network is now being recapitalised by the government, and this is precisely the type of recapitalisation that should be taking place, rather than harping on existing dysfunction— we need to move forward instead of looking back over our shoulder. Why has it taken us 20 years to realise this, and what is holding us back?

Just as the apartheid government imposed policies that were oppressive and destructive, so too is the ANC government proposing and enforcing policies that currently have and will continue to have a devastating effect on the country's economy. The economy is my number-one priority. If we don't protect it and enable it, how will we ever eradicate the extreme poverty that exists? One of the alarming proposed policies that will destroy South Africa is that of expropriating agricultural land.

The proposed appropriation of agriculture is a serious issue that needs serious thought. Why is the government proposing the appropriation of farms, creating uncertainty and fear, and ultimately intending to implement a plan that will destroy South Africa's agricultural industry? South Africa's most pressing problem is poverty alleviation. But appropriating farms will not alleviate poverty; it will further exacerbate the plight of the starving poor. Government has only to look over the border at Zimbabwe to see the results of expropriation of land. Prior to Robert Mugabe's land-grabbing exercise, Zimbabwe was the breadbasket of southern Africa. If the South African government persists in its proposed endeavour of appropriating agricultural land, the net result will be that we will end up importing our food, making it unaffordable to the already poor of our country.

There is no doubt that land reform is necessary, but the land reform strategy needs to be undertaken in a mature, measured, and controlled way. Is the government forging ahead with these plans unilaterally or engaging in discussions with farmers who have indicated that they are open to consultation and would be willing to develop the agricultural sector? Let's consider a scenario different from the one that the government proposes. Are there alternatives? Instead of alarming our food providers, can we look instead at the vast tracts of state-owned land that are underutilised, millions and millions of hectares of unused land? Could we consider taking up offers from farmers who are willing to sell their land for a reasonable price? Is it necessary to force farmers into relationships that will demotivate them, frustrate them, and result in their downfall? Instead, why don't we consider using free-market principles to create the right environment for a successful agricultural sector? The grim reality is that if we persist with an ill-devised plan to appropriate agricultural land to facilitate land reform, the agricultural sector will be destroyed. The economy will be paralysed. And, most concerning of all, it will be extremely difficult, if not impossible, to reactivate our agricultural sector, putting the cost of basic necessities well beyond the means of poor people.

Just as apartheid sought to enslave blacks economically, the ANC is doing so too in terms of its tripartite alliance with labour unions and the South African Communist Party. How is it possible to please labour and capitalists at the same time, which is what the government is currently trying to do? Government legislates to protect the labour component of the tripartite alliance, but it would do better if it tried to manage the exploitation of individual workers.

We have to create an environment that is conducive to business growth, instead of an environment that seeks to complicate it. If South Africa makes it difficult for small- and medium-sized businesses to exist because of over-legislation, it is not facilitating economic growth. The government is effectively paralysing the employment freedom guaranteed in our Constitution, by over-regulating business, by imposing a minimum wage, and by excluding certain groups from employment. As it is, many employees and employers are finding ways to work the system. It is not uncommon for an industrial workshop to get away with not paying minimum wage, not paying overtime, and reneging on bonus promises, and then when the union shop steward comes around for an inspection, the business owner simply puts a pile of cash into the shop steward's back pocket. The current policies are not working, and in no way do they protect the employees whom the government was mandated to protect. Businesses that are over-regulated will find a way around the rules, whereas if the government allowed employers and employees to contract freely, then the government could better serve the employed by ensuring that their conditions of employment are complied with—for example, in terms of safety equipment, medical care, and other easily trackable and practical conditions that will ensure the workers' welfare.

Instead of advancing the misguided notion of the 'evil' of capitalism, the government should be empowering people, giving them a helping hand to secure employment without laws that forbid and punish, and enabling them to provide for their families. The evil I see is not in capitalism but rather in the labour union and government alliance that privileges these interests such that they are 'fat-catting' themselves. The government constantly seeks to appease labour unions and keep communists happy, yet at the same time it runs a capitalist economy. How do you do that? It is not possible to be all things to all people, because in the process, you end up compromising the future and welfare of the majority of our people, the unemployed and unskilled. The high level of unemployment has reached unacceptable proportions, driven by our country's current dismal economic performance, in an economy that is constrained and restricted by government policy.

It has been more than 20 years since the ANC came to power, and it is beyond alarming that they are accelerating their policies to enslave and exploit. It is not what our first president, Nelson Mandela, and his comrades fought for, it is not what freed black people voted for, and it most certainly is not what all South Africans want. I will not stand by and watch South Africa brought to its knees by inefficient policies and the degeneration of governance.

CHAPTER 2

THE POWER OF OUR VOTES

Strong national policies and good governance are essential for the development of a healthy democracy; without them South Africa faces collapse on all levels. Fortunately, the South African Constitution was formulated and developed by top legal and social minds to provide for the human dignity of all South Africans, and is a remarkable democratic legislative framework for good governance. The Constitution came into effect in 1997 and really gave me a strong sense of national and social security, since I believed that by adhering to its provisions, South Africa was on a path of genuine, sustainable reform that would uplift its entire people and advocate good governance.

When Thabo Mbeki became president in 1999 I had a positive outlook on the future of the country, and my faith in the nation's leadership was cemented when Mbeki eloquently advocated and promoted what was commonly known as the African Renaissance initiative, whereby Africans strive to surmount African challenges to achieve economic, cultural, and scientific renewal; an initiative that I and many other people embraced. The rebirth of our continent under South Africa's leadership was an exciting prospect.

In 2000 the German government invited me to address a conference in Berlin to promote the African Renaissance initiative, which I understood under Mbeki's leadership to mean encouraging the continent to embrace the fundamental cornerstones of democracy, namely democratic principles, respect for the rule of law, and freedom of the press. Moeletsi Mbeki and Tokyo Sexwale were also among the speakers at the same conference.

However, my faith in Mbeki's leadership and his understanding of an African Renaissance were soon somewhat compromised when he supported (by his quiet diplomacy) Zimbabwe's land redistribution programme, a venture that resulted in massive human rights violations when white farmers were stripped of their farms without compensation, and often violently so. I felt betrayed and disappointed, and further events triggered serious doubts in me about Mbeki's political vision. In 2000 he appointed Jackie Selebi as the national police commissioner. In 2007 the National Prosecuting Authority (NPA) issued a warrant for Selebi's arrest on corruption charges. On the grounds of this investigation into Selebi, Mbeki placed him on extended leave in early 2008 and suspended Vusi Pikoli, head of the NPA. Mbeki's handling of Selebi's corruption and Pikoli's suspension raised serious questions in my mind regarding Mbeki's leadership and his lack of respect for the rule of law. How on earth could anyone justify maintaining the country's Commissioner of Police with a cloud of criminal cases hanging over his head? These doubts were extended to the ANC when they recalled Thabo Mbeki as president of the country in 2008, only three months before the national election; I realised I could no longer vote for the party of Mandela, Tambo, Sisulu and all the other leaders who had helped to deliver the freedom we were enjoying. Later, upon reading Reverend Frank Chikane's book *Eight Days in September: The Removal of Thabo Mbeki*, I got a sense of how the ANC was prepared and determined to expel Mbeki, again with brazen disregard for the rule of law. The rule of law must be paramount in a society that wishes to be considered democratic.

When the Congress of the People (COPE) was established as a result of Mbeki's expulsion, I was immediately suspicious of some members of its leadership, because it appeared that these individuals' motives were driven by personal advancement rather than an intention to serve the people of South Africa. The main mandate a political party receives when it wins an election is to adhere to the will of its constituents. Voters are guided by the principles and the policies that a political party promotes, and if a party advocates promoting the economy, I expect to see their policies aligned to such advocacy. When a party fails to deliver on its election promises, and appears to have other agendas, it is time to reconsider supporting that party.

Was it just me who was disgruntled with government policy in the run-up to the 2014 election? I engaged in conversations with friends and family, trying to gauge their political opinions and sentiment. I was encouraged that lengthy and vociferous political debate was taking place in my home-town of Hammanskraal, since I believe that without engage-ment, critical thinking cannot develop and there can be no hope of solutions for the country's problems. Even though I support everyone's right to vote for the party he or she supports, I was depressed by some of the opinions I heard.

Many of my friends and family, from young to old, seemed to feel that the Economic Freedom Front or the Democratic Alliance were best qualified to tackle the country's immediate local problems, such as employment or service delivery, be-cause the ANC had failed to deliver basic human services, and protests seemed to have had no effect. Yet these same people felt that they could not abandon the ANC nationally, and upon further probing, I saw that their support for the ANC on a na-tional level seemed to be motivated more by loyalty to the party that had delivered them from apartheid than by any belief that the ANC would actually deliver on promises. I drove home in a dark mood that night, dispirited by how sentimental allegiance might prevent the growth and development that South Africa so desperately needed. Just as I believe there is no place for emotion in the boardroom, I don't believe emotion has a place in elections. When voting, we really have the responsibility of voting for the party that represents our perspectives and will provide good governance.

In the build-up to the watershed 1994 election, I had taken some time off from my business and involved myself in voter education. As a member of the previously disenfranchised, I found that putting my cross on the ballot paper represented more than just supporting a political party. Like the majority of black South Africans, I was also voting for the first time in my life and recognised it for the momentous occasion it was going to be. We were exercising a right that had long been denied to us. Those who voted for the ANC were finally able to say *thank you, we believe in you to lead us into the new South Africa*. Undoubtedly, for many voters that first vote was going to be emotionally charged. However, I was adamant that people should understand what their votes meant, and I wanted to ensure that everyone who wanted to vote knew the procedure involved. Prior to that first democratic election, education was vital, since, like me, the majority of South Africans had never imagined ourselves being granted the freedom to vote, and we had little to no knowledge of voting protocols. My company Black Like Me funded a voter education programme run by Dr David Molapo of the I Can Foundation. David and his team, including his wife Mmamiki and Abner Mariri, did a sterling job across the country educating the educators. Many other organisations embarked on voter education campaigns. Despite these combined efforts to encourage voting, only 56.38% of the population were finally registered to vote; but what was inspiring was that 86.87% of those registered voters did indeed vote.

I need hardly describe the attendant euphoria. Every South African remembers. Images of long lines of eager and patient first-time voters swept through the media across every nation

		RECORD OF VOTING STATISTICS, 1994–2014			
Year	Voter Turnout	Population	Voting Age Population	Registered Voters	Total Vote
1994	86% (85%)	40 m	23 m	22 m	19 m
1999	89% (63%)	42 m	25 m	18 m	16 m
2004	76% (56%)	42 m	27 m	20 m	15 m
2009	77% (56%)	49 m	31 m	23 m	17m
2014	72% (60%)	48 m	31 m	25 m	18 m

Source: Adapted from www.idea.int/vt/countryview.cfm?CountryCode=ZA
Note: Voting age population turnout in parentheses.

during the three days of voting in this historic election. The whole world was celebrating with us as 19 million people voted for candidates in 19 political parties and the ANC swept to victory. Our votes were a hard-won freedom, but now voting is our right, and it deserves to be treated with mature thought and consideration for the future of our whole nation. As the 2014 election approached, I tried very hard to gauge South Africans' commitment to voting; after all, we can hardly criticise an administration if we do not participate in it at the most basic level, namely by voting.

In this voting statistics table it is evident that there are discrepancies between the South African population, the voting age population, the registered voters, and the number of people who actually cast their ballots. If we look at the 1994 election, the discrepancy between the recorded voting age population and registered voters is in the region of about a million.

If we analyse the results across the 20-year period, we can see that there has been a marked decline in the number of registered voters actually casting their votes (from a difference of 3 million in 1994 to a difference of 7 million in 2014 between registered voters and ballots cast). Indeed even more worrying, we see a significant decline in citizens registering to vote (25 million out of a population of 48 million). The decrease in registered voters is disturbing; our electoral responsibility has decreased from 86% to 72%, which means that almost 15% of electorally eligible people have renounced their civic responsibility. This will have severe repercussions on the administration of South Africa, since these voters are effectively leaving other people to decide their futures. While we can acknowledge that there are obvious valid reasons for not registering to vote—access to registration, illness, remoteness, lack of education, and fear of intimidation—a 15% abstention is high.

I wonder what this abstention is saying about the South African voting age population? Which segments of the population aren't registering to vote? Why aren't they registering to vote? Are they apathetic or frustrated? Have they given up or have they emigrated? Are they satisfied or dissatisfied with the way that South Africa is being governed? How do we even begin to assess this abstention? We need to engage with our fellow South Africans who don't vote and we need to examine their reasons for staying away from the polls, because votes are the way of ensuring that all voices are heard. Generations of South Africans never enjoyed this political freedom, and many suffered and died for this privilege. Not bothering to vote is both an apathetic shrug of one's political shoulders and an insult to those who fought to secure voting rights for all. It is also political myopia to refrain from voting, and it irresponsibly eliminates one's voice and one's say in the political future of our country. While a single vote might be a drop in the ocean, collectively votes have weight and can transform the direction a country takes.

The people and the policies that South Africans vote for determine the country's future. People who are against the government and refrain from voting are voiceless; their silences are not votes. Failure to vote will result in an administration that considers itself mandated by its population because of its policies. All the people who want to have a say in those policies must become responsible voters and must actively demand that their wishes be heard by voting for a party that will ensure the country is administered according to our Constitution. Being proactive and casting our votes means that we don't have the retroactive battle of challenging a government that strays; reactive and retroactive responses are ignored by government simply because when voters had the chance to challenge government or its policies, they were absent instead of seriously showing their commitment to how South Africa is administered. I think Pericles put it aptly: 'Just because you don't take an interest in politics doesn't mean politics won't take an interest in you.'

From the voting patterns shown in the preceding table, it would seem that voter education needs to be sustained and that it is as important now as it was in the run-up to our first democratic election. If South Africans hope to have any say in the country's administration and future, then we need to ensure that people vote, and we all need to know why we are voting and what the party we are voting for actually stands for, and what that party has delivered and what it intends to deliver.

As I engaged in conversations with fellow South Africans in the run-up to the 2014 election, I was frustrated with the responses from people who had decided to vote for the Economic Freedom Fighters (EFF) and the ANC. Why couldn't they see that the EFF was no better than the ANC, and that their economic policies, in particular their rhetoric about land expropriation without compensation and nationalisation of mines and banks, will certainly hurt the country? Why would anyone voluntarily support the ANC when it was led by a man refusing to face censure for his alleged corruption? How is it possible that our president managed to slip through the tight strictures of our Constitution? I tried to make sense of it. Was the ANC-led government's failure to respond to voters a reflection that the ANC was no longer in touch with what the citizens needed, and as a result some people felt that the EFF was the only party still in touch with their needs? On the other end of the political spectrum, why was the Democratic Alliance (DA) perceived as an elite white party that only had room for the *ja-baas* blacks? Did people consider the ANC government's misappropriation of the country's money to be acceptable because then the whites got less, or did ANC supporters view it as a time for blacks to feast? After 20 years, were we finally seeing what white people had been afraid of when the ANC came to power—that the white population would be side-lined in every sphere of society? Did marginalised black people want to see suffering for both whites and so-called *kleva* blacks (who look down on African ways and subscribe to middle-class individualism)? How had the country failed so spectacularly that these underlying racial issues were taking precedence in decision-making?

Surely when we vote we need to exhibit maturity and responsibility. But when I think about friends who basically have not worked since we left school 36 years ago, men and women who are only sporadically able to support their families, I can understand that they are hoping Julius Malema and the EFF will bring the plight and fight of the poor to the forefront of political agendas, that it is emotion and desperation that motivate their support of the EFF. Considering that it is the new political party on the block, the EFF did well. It managed to achieve an astounding 6% of the votes cast, more than a quarter of the votes secured by the official opposition, the DA (22%). And the EFF beat diehard parties such as the Inkatha Freedom Party (2%), the United Democratic Movement (1%) and the Pan Africanist Congress (0.21%). I can hardly blame EFF supporters who feel that the EFF is the only party talking to them, because as far as those unemployed and poor people living in dire circumstances are concerned, no other political party is saying anything to improve their situation. But this is all the EFF is doing too: talking. The party has not actually achieved anything except to incite disharmony and promote Mugabe-style land grabs. So what sector of the electorate is it to whom the EFF appeals—the genuine poor or the bone idle?

In the run-up to the 2014 election, and indeed since then, paging through the major newspapers reflects the signs of a government not coping, a government that has spiralled into dysfunction. A president being accused of allowing his alleged benefactors to land a plane at a national key point during wedding festivities, a president using R246 million of taxpay-ers' money to fund the upgrade on his personal property and refusing to repay the money despite the public protector's recommendation that he do so. Cabinet ministers giving jobs to pals and contracts to partners and family members, metro-politan cops trying to coerce motorists into buying e-tags on behalf of the South African National Roads Agency, parliamen-tarians and their wives accused of earning ghost salaries and drug-dealing, mismanagement and staff being exploited on mines owned by Broad-Based Black Economic Empowerment (BBBEE) companies. The allegations of corruption at every level and in every sector and the hardships suffered by the poor fill our newspapers. But amid all these depressing and infuriating news items, is there something positive that I am missing? Is the government's scorecard as poor as I imagined it is, and is that why people have stopped going to the polls—because they believe that their vote has no power to challenge or change government—or has the government achieved significant accomplishments that have given its supporters hope? Have the ANC actually delivered on the promises they made in their election manifestos?

Apartheid and its draconian policies systematically froze

out black people until the onslaught had dehumanised them. Are the ANC and its leadership flouting the Constitution and doing the same to anyone who challenges them—intimidating people and freezing them out? If South Africans don't demand adherence to the Constitution, namely democratic principles and adherence to the rule of law, where does our future lie? On the country's 20th anniversary of democracy it seems appropriate to perform a thorough investigation of the government's policies and adherence to the Constitution.

CHAPTER 3

CONSIDERING SOCIALISM

Every morning South Africans setting out for the day's work are confronted with dismaying realities. As traffic idles at the first major intersection near our homes, we encounter street vendors and beggars, all trying to eke out a daily living. A glance at the headlines forces us to think about the country's problems and issues: the EFF behind protests in Randfontein, Malamulela service delivery protests, racist practice in schools, the constitutional challenge by the Helen Suzman Foundation for the reinstatement of the head of the Gauteng Hawks, Selebi prosecutors to be investigated, the Eskom boss announcing the electricity crisis. Both the street vendors and the headlines reinforce my belief that in the years since the ANC came to power, South Africa has entered a state of substantial degeneration; degeneration that can only be ascribed to economic dysfunction and social disintegration. After more than 20 years of majority rule, one would expect that South Africa's new democracy would be nearing maturity, that we should see the country evolving democratically and following an established path of development and national stability. If this is not the case, then we need to look at who is governing the country, their policies, the administration of such policies, and how these policies are destabilising South Africa.

Since 1994 South Africa has effectively been governed by a tripartite alliance consisting of the ANC, the Congress of South African Trade Unions (COSATU), and the South African Communist Party (SACP). We all understand that this alliance was born at a time when the three groups had shared histories and shared aspirations. As a staff reporter for the online *Daily Maverick* noted: 'All three were led by self-sacrificing revolutionaries; people willing to lose life, limb and liberty for the freedom of all South African people. All three had members in prison and exile. All three had been the victims of a relentless onslaught from a cancerous minority and racist government of the National Party, whose viciousness was exacerbated by knowledge of its pending demise. All three were equally committed to ending white minority rule.'[1]

Since then, much has changed. South Africa has achieved majority rule and a strong Constitution. However, this political alliance has significantly influenced governmental policy and has serious continued implications for the nation's social and economic future. While many black South Africans have achieved financial security and indeed wealth over the past 20 years due to government policies that favour black empowerment, there are still millions of black South Africans trapped in poverty, their situation no better than it was during apartheid. Are the three arms of the tripartite alliance still pushing forward united in the noble ideals of their founders?

The ANC has been criticised for its failure to adhere to the values and integrity of its founding fathers. Factions within the ANC are striving for goals that are unaligned to the party's founding principles. Corrupt ministers abound, and personal agendas undermine national interests. The SACP appears to be nothing more than a puppet of the tripartite alliance, its most recent contribution to the puppet-masters having been its mobilisation by Jacob Zuma to oust the former president, Thabo Mbeki, in 2008 so that Zuma could become president. However, the SACP continues its outdated battle cry to nationalise the mining sector and the banking industry.[2] The SACP despises capitalists and continues to hold up a warped and false version of capitalism as a system intent on keeping the poor poor and inflating the income and influence of the wealthy. The SACP promotes its irrelevant and outdated 19th-century communist ideology to mislead the poor into believing that the communists support them. An EFF member recently tweeted that he was unable to identify a single communist within the SACP. I agree, since the SACP individuals who consistently preach their archaic communist ideology nevertheless indulge in extreme consumerism and enjoy lives of opulence that some capitalists, including myself, can only dream of.

COSATU's members have accused the organisation of losing focus and being ineffective. Ordinary members of the union accuse its leaders of using their positions in the union to further their own political careers instead of adhering to their office mandates. The 2012 Marikana mining tragedy is a case in point and is discussed later (see Chapter 6). Since Zuma's 2009 election, which was supported by COSATU, the trade union has failed abysmally in its political endeavours, facing defeat both in its youth wage subsidy attempts and in the effort to stop e-tolling. Yet its initiative to ban labour-broking seems to have found purchase and may soon succeed. COSATU has also experienced dissension in leadership struggles, with general secretary Zwelinzima Vavi experiencing personal scandals and finally dismissal from COSATU. It would appear that in spite of COSATU's support among millions of workers, the union does not have a strategy to harness members' support. Moreover, the union is frustrated in achieving the ideals of its support base because COSATU is restricted by its position in the tripartite alliance, having always to be in service to the ANC rather than of service to its members. A significant percentage of Zuma's cabinet is made up of former COSATU members. This latter point leads directly to why such a tripartite alliance is disastrous for South Africa's economy.

As an entrepreneur, I believe that a healthy economy underpins a nation's strength, and to this end I believe that capitalism and free markets are the only viable solution to help the country defeat our current inequalities, high unemployment, and extreme poverty. At the 24th Socialist International Congress in Cape Town in 2012, former Deputy President Kgalema

Motlanthe attributed poverty, increasing unemployment, and social inequality to 'the global crisis of capitalism and impe-rialism'.[3] I find it somewhat confusing that Motlanthe, as the deputy president of an arguably capitalist country, would sup-port a socialist agenda. For clarity about the two systems, it is perhaps opportune to draw some comparisons between them and how they are embodied in the South African context—because at the very foundation of a country's administration there should be agreement on what economic system and policies are implemented. We are indeed in danger if the ANC-led government can't decide whether it is implementing a capitalist system or a socialist one.

Many of our current government policies are decidedly so-cialist in nature. For example, the increased number of state employees has bloated the civil service, incurring outrageous costs that are a drain on the economy. According to the June 2013 Quarterly Employment Statistics published by Statistics South Africa (StatsSA), South Africa employed approximately 1.3 million civil servants.[4] At the end of Mbeki's presidency, there were 28 ministers. Zuma's 2014 cabinet consisted of 35 ministers and 37 deputy ministers. These superfluous minis-tries are a burden to our civil service bill, which grew by an outrageous 145.6% between 2005 and 2012.[5] Not only is the cost of this growth unsustainable, but the very serious fallout of a money-sucking civil service is that if it is allowed to continue, public sector spending priorities will be compromised. Eskom is a prime example of a collapsing public service that pays its top executives inflated salaries; in 2014 its former CEO Brian Dames was paid R14 million, plus bonuses, totalling R22.78 million.[6] Public service institutions are stuffed with employees who are keen to take home the money but less inclined to do the work necessary to keep their institutions on a solid footing. Bloating the public sector and inflating its salary bill is not job creation because it is not creating sustainable employment. It is simply a socialist intervention that creates an unmanageable strain on the public sector.

African-styled socialism is based on an all-powerful state controlled by dictators—presidents who use their countries and their institutions to serve themselves instead of their citizens. At present the South African president and many civil servants are abusing state funds to sponsor lifestyles of excess. Worse still is the official control of government contracts, especially where funds for such contracts are used to fund the ANC. The ANC, through its company Chancellor House, owns 25% of Hitachi Power Africa. Hitachi was awarded a lucrative Eskom contract to manufacture boilers for two power stations. The profits from these tenders are funnelled into the ANC party coffers.[7]

Socialism promotes government ownership and control, and any economic sector that is dominated by the government is socialist in nature, irrespective of whether that government officially considers itself to follow other social or economic systems. Even successful social democratic Scandinavian countries have changed tack and are realising the weight of a financially draining public service. Adrian Wooldridge reports in

The Economist: 'The [Danish] welfare state ... is excellent in most ways,' says Gunnar Viby Mogensen, a Danish historian. 'We only have this little problem. We can't afford it.'[8] To remedy this, the Nordic governments are updating their version of capitalism to cope in a more challenging global environment. 'They continue to believe in combining open economies with public investment in human capital. But the new Nordic model begins with the individual rather than the state.'[9]

Deputy President Motlanthe's apportioning blame to capitalism is unfounded and inaccurate with regard to the 'global crisis of capitalism and imperialism' that he mentioned. This international crisis—reaching well beyond the meltdown of 2008—is not the result of private banks acting irresponsibly but rather of central banks doing so. The financial crisis is the result of mismanagement of currencies by central banks that are or were controlled by the governments of the various countries. It is these governments that established central bank monopoly control over currency issues because they did not believe that private banks could be trusted to manage currencies. The crisis is a failure of socialist currency and fiscal mismanagement, definitely not a failure of capitalism. The solution is for governments to stop spending more than they receive and for central banks to stop reducing the value of their currencies by printing too much money. The solution is less socialism and more capitalism.[10]

The South African government's antipathy towards and criticism of capitalism has its roots in colonialism, West vs

East during the Cold War, and of course apartheid. During the apartheid South Africa into which I was born and in which I operated my business, I was confined to economic activity that was allowed according to my race and the geographical areas where I could legally work. According to apartheid policy, if you farmed pigs, you could only sell your pork through the Pork Board, and price control was exercised on everything from wheat to petrol. National monopolies were encouraged, completely cutting out small private enterprises in sectors such as steel, coal, and the gold and diamond industries. These monopolies persist today whereby bargaining councils prevent the small entrepreneur from participating in some sectors of the economy. The Nationalist government strictly controlled the media. Television was not introduced until 1976 because the government was terrified of its potential power, and even then it was completely controlled by limiting transmission to a single government-owned broadcaster, the South African Broadcasting Corporation. These are not aspects of capitalism, which is what the ANC believes existed during apartheid; these are aspects of fascism reminiscent of Italy and Germany in the 1930s. So do South Africans who rail against capitalism even know what capitalism is?

The ANC government does not recognise that capitalism in its true sense, its pure form, is not about exploitation and greed and nationalisation but about creating work opportunities, promoting free markets, elevating the workforce, and establishing a healthy, competitive economy. I agree with economist Mike

Schüssler, who suggests that there is 'much [in South Africa] that does not support the fight against capitalism'.[11] Among his reasons, he cites home ownership, household size, transport mobility, savings, and company ownership as signs that 'South Africa is more of a capitalist state than most European countries'.[12] He claims that we have one of the highest home ownership rates in the world. In 2013 more than 62% of South African households owned their home or were paying it off. This translates to more than nine million homeowners or 18% of the population. Home ownership, certainly a characteristic of capitalism, is on the rise in South Africa: 'Nine times more Africans have a fully paid-off home than Whites. A third of Africans also own a second home—the highest rate in the world today that I could find.'[13] Household size has dropped from 4.8 to 3.4 people, which is 'another indicator of wealth, as higher household formation growth than population growth occurs mainly in richer countries'.[14] Additionally, passenger-car ownership is extremely high, with eight million cars and bakkies on the road and 200 000 minibus taxis in the informal sector.

Schüssler adds that 16 million South Africans have bank savings and 9.4 million contribute to a pension fund or other savings products. 'The value of pension funds, life insurance and unit trusts amounts to more than R5 trillion.'[15] Slightly more than 810 000 South Africans own unit trusts, and 340 000 own shares, while 1.5 million people are beneficiaries of BEE ownership schemes. 'This means formal workers are major owners of the means of production. Pension [funds] generally own shares of the largest companies, shopping malls and government debt, etc. About 40% of the JSE is owned by pension funds on behalf of employees.' South African policy dictates employee share ownership, benefitting more than a million employees, representing 'one of the highest participation rates in the world'.[16]

Considering the scenario I have described, it is evident that ownership is prevalent in South Africa, and ownership is not a socialist characteristic. Instead it is representative of capitalism and a free market. Why then does the government not recognise this and refrain from implementing or mooting socialist policies that will derail the functioning and vibrant aspects of capitalism? Is it because many ANC comrades falsely link capitalism to white political supremacy, harking back to the days of Rhodes, Barnato, Oppenheimer and the De Beers, where there is no doubt that white interests were protected while black people were heartlessly exploited in the mining industry? Is the criticism of capitalism based on emotion or fact? This is the question that the opponents of capitalism need to ask themselves if they really have South African interests at heart. Currently these critics are throwing the baby out with the bath water at great cost to the country.

We have to acknowledge that, since 1994, state intervention has increased, the government has increased the number of state employees significantly, land redistribution is again going to be imposed, and we have created a welfare state with almost 16 million people now receiving state grants. I am a strong supporter of state intervention for the less privileged, pensioners, and physically and mentally challenged people. But social welfare practice has to be an intervention, not a permanent feature of human life and existence, and in South Africa this is not always the case. For example, millions of young people have been seduced by social grants, which has resulted in a shameful welfare system whereby youths are rewarded for bearing children (see Chapter 4). Such a system is intrinsically socialist in nature, since the risk of having to work has been reduced, and people are rewarded for doing nothing. This is a terrible blow to the economy; the hunger of the entrepreneurial spirit has been satisfied by a handout, resulting in a depressed and under-educated workforce, to say nothing of the lack of elevation of our people.

The government's Twenty Year Review for 1994–2014 would have us believe that South Africa is a vibrant democracy. While the review admits to ongoing challenges, which are normal, it also presents and indeed omits scenarios that should not go unchallenged. By challenging the government's policies, my intention is not to denigrate the accomplishments that have been achieved but rather to illuminate and analyse the implications of their policies and administration in terms of a developing democracy according to the Constitution.

According to the intention of the Twenty Year Review, the government seeks to 'reflect on the legacy that democratic South Africa inherited, how the country has progressed in realising the objectives it set for itself in 1994, the challenges that still remain and how we could best address these as we enter the third decade of democracy'.[17] During the run-up to the 2014 national elections the ANC commissioned this major report as it sought to highlight its policy achievements since 1994. (A review since 2009 would have shown far fewer signs of initiative or responsibility.)

A large portion of the Twenty Year Review concerns the inheritance of the 48-year apartheid regime, a bleak reminder of those oppressive times that cannot be ignored. However, I sincerely hope that the government will not spend the next 20 years continuing to look over its shoulder into the distant past and blaming its own failure to progress on the restrictive policies of a regime that no longer exists. It is certainly time for the government to stand on the record of its own time in power and accept criticism that has evolved from ANC policies and administrations instead of from those of the apartheid government. I believe that in order to progress, we need to keep our eyes forward on the common goal of national development and growth.

It is through the lens of the Constitution, my personal business experiences, and my high regard for capitalism—which despite socialist tinges is essentially the successful economic system under which South Africa operates—that certain policies and achievements over the past two decades are examined in the following chapters.

CHAPTER 4

PAYING FOR THE SAFETY NET

I grew up in poverty without knowing where our next meal was coming from, or, worse still, knowing there wasn't going to be a meal that night. Such circumstances spark one of three things within people—you become despondent, bitter or determined. I experienced all three emotions, but ultimately it was determination, partnered by opportunity and hard work, or sometimes both, that helped me to escape the poverty trap. However, I understand that lack of food and opportunities and the struggle for life can be completely energy-sapping and can leave people choked in despair.

In any major South African metropolitan area we are squarely confronted by the scale of poverty that exists in our country. We have all witnessed mothers sitting wearily begging with their toddlers at busy intersections, crippled beggars limping along on crutches, and teenagers spraying water onto your windscreen, hoping for a few rand for their trouble. A little lower on the desperation ladder are droves of hawkers desperate to sell everything from a car licence holder to a plastic rosary—anything that might prompt motorists to open their windows and their wallets. These street dwellers and workers are the hopeful yet visible poor who confront South Africans daily, although they are by no means the majority of the poor in our country.

New industrial suburbs are boomed off, and security guards are selective in the pedestrians they allow through the gates because business owners don't want unemployed men and women clutching tools or CVs loitering outside companies or knocking on doors looking for work.

One only has to drive further out of the cities to confront the vast poverty that is the daily reality of many, many South Africans, black and white. People are squashed into makeshift shacks that leak in the rainy months and admit frigid winter winds. Yet even in these communities, where there is little to no running water, no sanitation, and no municipal service delivery, entrepreneurs pop up, determined to eke out an existence through the sale of a few sweets, a minimal fee for phone charging, or roasted smileys (sheep heads) to feed grumbling bellies—an informal economy that sustains the poorest people of all. Let us consider the men and women I have regularly referred to as scavengers, those we see every morning in our suburbs going through our dustbins searching for anything from bottles to other items that they may be able to sell. These people wake up every morning at around three or four so as to be first to go through the suburban dustbins. They have to push trolleys alongside peak traffic for kilometres, earning perhaps about R60 to R80 a day.

Why am I raising the matter of these self-driven South Africans? Because of their determination to work and provide for their families. What concerns me about their plight is the government rhetoric regarding decent jobs and minimum salaries. Is waste-picking one of the decent jobs that the government is talking about? What about our women, young and old, mothers and fathers and boys and girls, car-washing in shopping centres? What skills are these poor people gaining from such activity? What about the psychological and social effects of working in these unhygienic and dignity-destroying circumstances? Are these scavengers proud to tell their children and families where they work and what type of work they do, or are they isolated from family and society? A government sincerely committed to effective eradication of poverty should at least allow these people to be employed by small business, to gain the necessary experience to move up the employment ladder.

Poverty is a serious issue that plagues all developing countries. In 1994, in the Reconstruction and Development Programme, the government stated that 'no political democracy can survive and flourish if the mass of our people remain in poverty, without land, without tangible prospects for a better life ... attacking poverty and deprivation must therefore be the first priority of a democratic government', and these objectives were echoed in the 2011 National Development Plan.[1] In its Medium Term Strategic Framework the government intended to 'halve poverty and unemployment by 2030'.[2] Noble intentions, no doubt, because poverty is not only ethically unacceptable; it is also devastating to our economy and our sociopolitical security and stability. Exactly how has the government tackled poverty eradication? According to its Twenty Year Review, 'social assistance through grants has been the democratic government's *most effective poverty-reduction tool*'.[3] The number of grant beneficiaries increased from 2.7 million people in 1994 to more than 16 million people by 2013.[4]

Social assistance is essential, and as earlier noted I am fully supportive of such assistance, but I prefer to consider social assistance as an intervention measure as opposed to our current experience. The elderly and disabled in our communities do need pensions to survive. Undoubtedly, the raw reality of AIDS is that there are thousands and thousands of child-headed households that would be unable to survive without financial support. Social grants provide a necessary safety net for these vulnerable members of our society, but not all such assistance falls into acceptable categories.

It hurts me deeply to see female children, from as young as 14 years old, effectively being turned into pensioners. When the policy of providing young mothers with government grants was instituted, critics suggested that the practice would become a business, and I immediately brushed this criticism aside. I couldn't fathom that a human being could have a child simply for the sake of money. Unfortunately, today it is an accepted practice in some communities for some women under the age of 20 to have two to three children from different fathers. Some of these women don't even know who has fathered their children. You can just imagine the social impact of such a practice on the country in years to come. This social welfare policy is destroying the self-worth of our children—children who are our country's future. I consider the system of turning young girls into pensioners due to early pregnancies an abhorrent practice. The government should be focusing its policies on the education of these children instead of encouraging them to make babies. I initially supported this social grant programme and rejected the notion that young people would become parents for a mere R180 a month, but let's take a look at social grant allocations since their implementation.

An overview of the South African Social Security Agency statistical report shows an expectable range of social grants for war veterans, old-age pensioners, disability pensioners, etc. However, when it comes to the child support grant, the grant given to teenage parents, the figures are staggering—more than 11.5 million recipients received these grants in 2014. Why such substantial numbers, resulting in an enormous amount of money allocated to these grants? This statistic attests to a situation where we are essentially creating a state of child pensioners, and that in itself is grievous. And there are other questions. Is this money reaching the very children it is intended to reach? Is there any substance to the rumours that young women are having children to access this money?

Even more alarming is that if we analyse the grant totals, they are increasing significantly over time. The number of

NUMBER OF SOCIAL GRANTS BY GRANT TYPE AND REGION,

31 OCTOBER 2014

	GRANT TYPE							
Region	OAG	WVG	DG	GIA	CDG	FCG	CSG	TOTAL
EC	523,793	53	182,308	14,724	18,900	123,805	1,844,097	2,707,680
FS	179,631	6	77,172	1,772	6,281	43,449	649,301	957,612
GP	467,898	90	113,765	2,582	15,955	60,519	1,625,722	2,286,531
KZN	623,367	46	293,916	34,858	36,144	137,848	2,754,318	3,880,497
LP	426,550	25	93,557	17,086	13,016	64,051	1,683,344	2,297,629
MP	222,334	16	78,968	4,478	9,336	37,453	1,023,427	1,376,012
NC	78,157	10	50,214	6,180	4,752	15,466	286,853	441,632
NW	229,616	12	86,130	6,488	8,851	42,242	787,548	1,160,887
WC	285,368	104	155,449	11,210	11,720	31,241	918,180	1,413,272
TOTAL	3,036,714	362	1,131,479	99,378	124,955	556,074	11,572,790	16,521,752

Source: Social pension system, South African Social Security Agency[5]

Legend: OAG = Old Age Grant, WVG = War Veterans Grant, DG = Disability Grant, GIA = Grant in Aid, CDG = Child Dependency Grant, FCG = Foster Child Grant, CSG = Child Support Grant

social grant beneficiaries has doubled from 7.9 million in 2003 to 16.5 million in 2014, and this increase is mainly ascribed to the increase in the child support grants, which now amount to nearly three-quarters of all these social assistance grants.[6] Let me reiterate the earlier statement that 'social assistance through grants has been the democratic government's *most effective poverty-reduction tool*.[7] If this is the situation, then South Africa is on a completely unsustainable path to eradicate poverty. What actual effect does R12.50 per day per child have on eradicating poverty? That represents just one loaf of bread a day and ignores all the other needs of a child—access to health care, education, transport, and housing.

So one has to ask, on the basis of R12.50 a day, how does a child afford to go to school? Living on a loaf of bread a day, how does a child concentrate sufficiently to acquire knowledge and skills? How does a child get books, uniforms, and transport to school on that sum? For many families, child care grants are not an additional resource for child rearing—they're the only resource. Most families who receive child grants are unemployed, so the R380 a month isn't merely insufficient; it's insulting to them, and is it possibly just an ANC-inspired strategy to keep the hungry believing in the party's election promises?

The government's current school feeding system providing free meals to '3.5 to 5 million school children' is another social handout that does not contribute to poverty eradication.[8] A high level of corruption exists in the allocation of tenders to feed these children, and the cost is significant. Additionally, the manner in which these poor children are fed unfortunately lowers their self-esteem. You do not have to be a social scientist to be aware of the soul-destroying results of such feeding schemes. Parents send their kids to school to acquire education, not to be fed. The government should focus on making it easy for these children's parents to work and to be proud and responsible providers. Instead, the government undermines their dignity by frustrating their employability and making them reliant on handouts.

Where is the government transport that conveys an 85-year-old person to the social grant pay point? Where is the bus to transport children? Where are the jobs that allow parents to earn money to feed their children so that they aren't too malnourished to think? What social services provide support so that children can do homework, instead of spending their afternoons caring for younger orphaned siblings, or stealing wood from a nearby farm to keep their shack warm? The non-alignment of poverty alleviation strategies exhibits a shotgun approach, instead of an intensive and focused approach to ensure that all sectors facilitate poverty alleviation.

According to StatsSA, the drop in poverty levels can be attributed to 'a growing social safety net, income growth, above inflation wage increases, decelerating inflationary pressure and an expansion of credit'.[9] This statement is made up of contradictory elements. For instance, you can't expand your social grants and still expect business to pay higher salaries, take smaller profits, and continue to invest in a country. Indeed, not even the government's Public Investment Company (PIC) would invest in a company that did not try to achieve profits. The PIC has invested in many companies, yet I am not aware of a single instance where the PIC has invested in a listed company that has stated its intended objective as 'to pay higher salaries'. It's a ludicrous scenario. Business, in particular small business, has to be allowed to operate in an environment where employers pay what they can afford and have a workforce willing to accept selling their labour at this agreed price.

Expansion of personal credit has also had a crushing effect on business, with African Bank being a recent case in point. This bank lent billions to clients who couldn't honour their payments. Extending credit facilities to expand business is valid and good, but providing credit to increase personal debt is absolutely not a healthy sign in an economy. If money is being borrowed to create opportunities and build businesses, that's healthy, but lending to fund the purchase of trendy Nike trainers, to fund excessive consumerism, is irresponsible. Of course consumerism spurs the economy, but at what cost to the consumer?

As already mentioned, a growing social safety net is completely unsustainable in the long term. Someone has to pay for the social safety net, and if a small section of the population is heavily taxed, the situation becomes untenable. Real income growth would contribute to poverty alleviation, but for real income growth you need to encourage entrepreneurs and new businesses—you can't just have above-inflation wage increases. This is the very problem that I have with the current system of bargaining councils: they extend their irresponsible, one-size-fits-all policy to certain industries. On one hand, the central bank governor is trying to decrease inflation, but, on the other hand, some elements of the tripartite alliance are contributing to inflation by having above-inflation wage increase demands.

Every industry is unique, every job type is unique; you can't just have blanket criteria for industries. If the gold price returns to what it was six to eight years ago, and the bargaining councils have committed to five-year increases in above-inflation wages, the mines will be forced to close up shop. The Aurora gold mine is a good example of this. The mine was not making money, and sometimes businesses are worth more when they're closed down than when they're operating—worth more to asset strippers, that is. Aurora mine was stripped of all assets, and the workers were never paid.

Against this backdrop of unsustainable social grants and intrusive legislation, we should look again at the tripartite alliance in the context of managing the economy to fight the three areas identified as pressing challenges facing the country, namely high unemployment, poverty, and inequality. Members of the alliance do not all share the same agenda. On the face of it the labour movement represented by COSATU appears to drive the agenda to gain the best deals for its members, which is a fair and proper route to pursue. Although the SACP is supposed to be the vanguard party for the poor and vulnerable, nobody in the country can tell what this party represents today. And the ANC, which is supposed to be the major partner within this structure, seems reluctant to engage in discourse on economic policies. COSATU and the SACP are the only vocal entities that debate economic issues, very often with standpoints contrary to statements made by the government itself. Currently the government talks about the National Development Plan as its official economic policy, asking for buy-in and commitment from business, yet at the same time we have certain members within COSATU rejecting this plan. It is unfortunate to have this tripartite alliance internally at odds and tearing itself apart regarding the key elements for facilitating the country's economic growth. It is also impossible to know who is driving economic policy.

To reduce poverty, companies need to start investing their resources and profits in the country, but to do so they require stability, opportunities, infrastructure and certainty. Currently the private sector sits on billions of rand in cash reserves that are simply not being reinvested. Why? Because the government is not providing an environment conducive to encouraging investment in South Africa. A case in point is the government's failure to deliver an efficient and sufficient electricity supply to the economy. When Eskom initially brought this risk to government attention in 1998, the warnings were ignored until the lights eventually went off in 2008. Delays in the establishment of the Medupi coal-fired power station are indeed an alarming situation. To meet their commitments, businesses are forced to invest heavily in generators to address the electricity shortage occasioned by mismanagement and failure to invest in the country's infrastructure. Due to their financial constraints, small businesses cannot afford such luxuries. Unfortunately South Africa is currently viewed by the investment community as being unfriendly towards business.

The government is failing to identify global trends and has

not facilitated infrastructure that is vital for kick-starting economic growth. In fact, the government needs to refrain from its Big Brother business intervention and allow the private sector to function without interference so that it can play its role in job creation. Entrepreneurs are savvy. They will always identify opportunities where these exist and are prepared to take the necessary risks associated with their plans. Creating the right environment for entrepreneurs to do business should be the government's focus; the government should not be dictating to businesses and should refrain from passing a barrage of laws preventing entrepreneurial activity.

What steps should the government take to promote a healthy and vibrant business environment that sees companies being successful and employment being available to all who want to work? A key ingredient in creating the right environment for business is the application of the rule of law. Business needs to operate in an environment where the rule of law is respected and enforced. Government can provide infrastructure, such as upgrading the rail network and building the Medupi power station. This type of government commitment will foster confidence, encourage entrepreneurs, and create new business. The government also needs to identify global trends and facilitate infrastructure around these economies, as well as change the economy by identifying opportunities to become a knowledge-based economy rather than a resource-based economy.

As an example, entrepreneurs identified our excellent English-speaking population as an asset and created businesses such as call centres, where good English is a prerequisite, bringing South Africa into the modern world economy. The tourism industry is another huge employment opportunity for South Africa. Our apartheid history attracts foreign tourists to the country. Our sublime climate allows visitors to enjoy our country throughout the year, and we offer superb national parks, excellent clean beaches, and world-class golfing facilities across the country. Such trends and opportunities need to be identified, and the government can facilitate the infrastructure around that economy, instead of taking industries that are struggling in terms of global competitiveness—that is, clothing and textiles, metal manufacturers, and car manufacturers—and pushing them to the edge so that they either move their operations offshore or close down, because there is a limit to what companies can do. Creating the right environment to encourage entrepreneurs, like myself, and facilitating the ease of doing business will result in a situation where companies will make profits and jobs will be created—undoubtedly the best poverty alleviator, nationally and internationally.

CHAPTER 5

JOBS, RIGHTS AND LAWS

Reflecting back on my upbringing and the unemployment levels in my environment, I grew up where every
able-bodied person who wanted to work was working. Babelegi
industrial area, established by the apartheid government in
the early seventies to keep and attract black people within the
homeland structures, provided employment opportunities for
the communities in the greater Hammanskraal area. Our parents, families, and neighbours woke up every morning and
went to work. Some people regarded those factories as exploitation machines, but some took advantage to provide for
their families and to improve their lives. We cannot deny that
there was exploitation. The apartheid government was directly
responsible for that by denying people trade union representation. When the ANC came to power in 1994, I was excited and
convinced that the huge barriers that had existed to repress
black entrepreneurs and black business had been dismantled,
that South Africa would see a significant rise in black business,

that entrepreneurship would flourish and therefore employment would rise.

On its website the Department of Labour states its official
vision as striving 'for a labour market which is conducive to investment, economic growth, employment creation and decent
work'. It means to 'play a significant role in reducing unemployment, poverty and inequality through a set of policies and
programmes developed in consultation with social partners,
which are aimed at:

- ☐ Improved economic efficiency and productivity.
- ☐ Employment creation.
- ☐ Sound labour relations.
- ☐ Eliminating inequality and discrimination in the
  workplace.
- ☐ Alleviating poverty in employment'.[1]

The Department of Labour constantly informs us that South
Africa's labour laws are not responsible for our chronic unemployment. Yet my personal experience shows otherwise.
Unemployment on the grand scale that we have in South Africa
is unnatural; it must have a cause.

The government's Twenty Year Review states: 'Higher levels of education have gone hand in hand with changes in the
structure of employment. Employment of workers classed as
managerial, professional or semi-professional increased most
rapidly, followed by clerical and sales work, which typically

requires matric. These occupations climbed around 3% a year from 1994 to 2013, while employment of elementary and semi-skilled workers rose by just over 1.5% a year. Employment of elementary workers was affected by the decline in domestic and agricultural work through the 1990s and early 2000s, although both sectors saw job growth from the mid 2000s. Finally, skilled production workers (including artisans) dropped from 12% of total employment in 1994 to 11% in 2013.[2] The percentages bandied about here are minor over the relevant time period and prove that no significant progress has been made to address the unacceptably high levels of unemployment, especially among skilled workers.

Despite apartheid legislation barring blacks from business activity, entrepreneurship was always a key characteristic of township life during apartheid; anybody who could turn a profit with a carton of cigarettes or a crate of bananas did so. That entrepreneurial drive still exists, but government policies now thwart it at every turn. Local municipal authorities systematically raid vendors on street corners and outside shopping centres and confiscate their goods, effectively shutting down entrepreneurship and stifling self-sufficiency, leaving a massive chunk of the population in dire economic straits. In my view and experience, the strict and complicated labour laws effectively prevent small business operators in the townships from complying with labour laws. A salon owner in the township had her salon shut down by authorities because she could not afford to pay her employees the minimum wage that government insists upon, even though those employees were willing to work so that they could survive. As a result of this type of intrusion, bureaucratisation and labour laws are destroying the spirit of entrepreneurship in the country.

Unemployment in South Africa is horrific. Recent statistics reveal that the number of unemployed people increased over the second quarter of 2014 to '5.2 million, the highest level since the inception of the [Quarterly Labour Force Survey] in 2008'.[3] This does not include those people who have effectively given up work and are no longer actively seeking employment; thus the real rate of unemployment affects a staggering 8.3 million people.[4] Behind this overwhelming statistic are human beings who live in our communities across the country, and very many of them are young people whose aspirations and livelihoods are being destroyed by unemployment. A significant portion of the unemployed population is under the age of 25.

With the democracy in place today, and the right to belong to a trade union of your choice, the government should be encouraging and incentivising business establishment in areas like Hammanskraal, Ga-Rankuwa, Qwaqwa, etc. The advantage of such places is that they are in, or are close to, densely populated areas that should be used as catalysts to launch and advance people's career options. But to do this, we need the political leadership with a vision and strong desire to see people advance in their lives. People can only improve their lives when they have family stability. Family stability happens when parents provide for their children and teach them the value of hard work. Family stability happens when parents work and live side by side with their children. The government has the responsibility to create such an environment for its citizens.

By 2012 I felt that changes in government policies had not resulted in the dynamic growth in business and entrepreneurship that I had envisaged, and the economic degeneration of the country spurred me into allying myself with the Free Market Foundation (FMF) because I could no longer be a bystander to the economic chaos, the joblessness and the hopelessness being experienced by fellow South Africans. My concern with the plight of vulnerable small and medium enterprises (SMEs), entrepreneurs, and desperate unemployed people had compelled me to join this foundation in 2006, culminating in taking over as the chairman in 2012. My involvement with the FMF is more fully described in Chapter 7.

To me one of the most alarming issues is that of the unemployed youth. Kevin Lings, chief economist at STANLIB, states that the rate of the unemployed youth stands 'at an incredible 66%'.[5] The World Economic Forum's Global Risks 2014 report states: 'South Africa has the third highest unemployment rate in the world for people between the ages of 15 to 24 ... 52% of young people in South Africa are unemployed, which is four times the figure for sub-Saharan Africa.'[6] Lyndy van den Barselaar, MD of Manpower South Africa, stresses the need to 'create a workforce that is in line with the country's needs in terms of required skills for existing and growing industries'.[7] She adds that it is important for all parties to be informed 'about how the country's business landscape is evolving and what skills are in demand' to ensure that we have the appropriate skills required by the South African economy.[8]

This assertion is corroborated by StatsSA, which also notes this further problem: 'Young people who are employed are more likely to be employed in precarious conditions; for example 20.7% of employed youth are on contracts of a limited duration compared to 10.8% of employed adults.'[9] These are facts I know to be true, since 26- and 28-year-old members of my family have never had a job; their matric certificate simply is not sufficient, and they don't have skills.

The very real danger of a high population of unemployed youths is evident in the Jasmine Revolution that started in Tunisia in 2012 when 26-year-old Mohammed Bouazizi could not find a job after graduating. Refusing to join the 'army of unemployed youth', he started a small business as a street vendor, selling vegetables to support his family. A police officer seized his produce, claiming that Bouazizi did not have the necessary hawking permit. The young man complained to a centre for unemployed graduates, but his protest was ignored, and in a state of absolute desperation, on 17 December 2010, Bouazizi set fire to himself in front of a government building. He died 18 days later in hospital.

Khadija Cherif, who works for the Paris-based International Federation for Human Rights, said Bouazizi was a 'symbol for all the young college graduates who were unemployed, and [...] was a sort of catalyst for the violent demonstrations which followed'.[10] This incident triggered a revolution across North African and Middle Eastern countries and should surely be a dire warning to the South African government to give immediate attention to the overwhelming numbers of unemployed youths.

The Free Market Foundation has proposed time and again that the only solution to the severe unemployment problem is to eliminate the labour laws that remove the rights of the unemployed. What are some of these labour laws that are contributing to the high levels of unemployment?

According to the government's Twenty Year Review: 'The Labour Relations Act of 1995 introduced organisational rights for workers, set a framework for bargaining structures, provided for alternative dispute settlement in labour relations and the Commission for Conciliation, Mediation and Arbitration (CCMA), and regulated dismissals for operational reasons, as well as for poor productivity and disciplinary offences. The Labour Relations Act sought to protect workers from the kind of arbitrary and unfair dismissals that many had experienced under apartheid. Specifically, the Labour Relations Act aimed to do the following:

- ☐ Minimise costs and delays, and reduce the legal costs of settling disputes.
- ☐ Encourage sectoral bargaining councils to respond to sectoral needs, which includes setting minimum pay and benefits, and settling disputes, within the framework of national law.

☐ Promote collaboration between employers and
workers at the workplace level by providing for
workplace forums.

☐ Avoid the highly legal and procedural approach to
dismissals.

☐ Protect workers' organisations as crucial for fair and
effective bargaining.'[11]

The important aspects in the Labour Relations Act are the CCMA
(Commission for Conciliation, Mediation and Arbitration) and
the protection of the bargaining councils, and they cannot go unchallenged if we seek to address and improve unemployment.

In 1998, when I was still actively running Black Like Me, I
visited a major client in Polokwane (Pietersburg) with whom I
had a mutually beneficial relationship dating back to the 1980s
when I started the company. We developed more than a pro-
vider–client relationship, and while my regional sales team
was responsible for his account, he and I would often discuss
business growth and strategies and share information about
competitors. During this visit, he advised me that it was
necessary to employ a full-time Black Like Me merchandiser
in his store to stock and replenish the shelves and to advise
consumers about our products. I approved of his idea and
agreed that it would be a good investment to hire someone.
My client recommended two possible female candidates, and
I explained the position to the two women and asked them to
provide their contact details for me to pass on to my regional

manager, so that he could make the necessary arrangements to interview them for the position. I duly passed on their contact information and left matters in my manager's capable hands.

Two months later I was surprised to receive a notice from the CCMA to appear at a hearing in Polokwane. I was confused about the notice and asked the human resources manager of Black Like Me to make enquiries regarding the allegation. We established that one of the candidates my client had recommended had claimed I had 'assured' her she would be employed in the position and that I had reneged on my word. Since I had given no such assurance, I immediately contacted the CCMA commissioner in charge of the case and explained the situation. I was advised to make a written statement to avoid being personally summonsed to appear in Polokwane. My statement was duly dismissed, and I was then advised to appear in person to avoid judgment being entered against me. On the advice of professional HR practitioners, I made three appearances in Polokwane. The commissioner attempted to persuade me to settle out of court to avoid the case dragging on, but I refused to compromise and settle, and eventually I won the case.

This experience was illuminating. I had expected the commissioners to act in a fair and just manner to promote a healthy employment environment for both employees and employers, but the experience taught me otherwise. I was annoyed at the CCMA's abuse of power, trying to bully me into settlement just to avoid wasting time.

A few years later, I witnessed an SME destroyed by CCMA practices because the business owners had neither the knowledge nor the capacity to deal with the CCMA's complex legal requirements. The business owners' legal ignorance and lack of resources cost them their hard-earned business. The government and Department of Labour do not care about the plight of business owners; their sole concern is the protection of employees.

The CCMA was established with the intention of resolving labour disputes between employers and employees, but many employers, myself included, believe that the CCMA protects only the rights of the worker. Let's take the scenario of a small business. In terms of the CCMA's Code of Good Practice on Dismissals, the onus is on the employer to prove that an employee is incapable, under all reasonable scenarios, of performing adequately in the job, or that an employee has consistently and wilfully withheld his or her performance. The employer is obliged to provide training, to recruit the employee correctly, to have explicit performance standards in place, among many other obligations, before the CCMA will consider a dismissal for poor performance. The employee, by contrast, has very few reciprocal obligations in practice and 'many employees shrug off their workplace duties and hide behind the law, in which situation employers are helpless'.[12]

If workers consider themselves unfairly dismissed and seek to address their dismissal through the CCMA, the SME owner often does not have available either the legal resources or the time that a large corporation has to fight a case of unfair dismissal. Many small businesses and private employers have

chosen not to employ individuals simply because they fear being taken to the CCMA. In order to compensate for the loss of
physical labour, they can mechanise, or do the work themselves,
or employ a foreigner who has no redress through the CCMA,
rather than employing someone who might take them to the
CCMA, or they can close their businesses. Whichever option
these business owners adopt, the result has serious implications
for South Africa's future.

It would be ignorant to assume that legitimate cases are not
brought before the CCMA. However, private or small employers are not willing to become entangled in bureaucracy, and nor
do they have the financial and legal resources to engage in disputes. And unfortunately, in some cases, the way around having
to face this scenario is to employ and even exploit foreign workers, which in turn has its implications for employment and the
labour legislation working against itself. The strategy of using
foreign workers creates serious conflicts with the unemployed
locals, a situation we need to guard against as a country. The
xenophobic cases experienced in some townships from 2008 to
2015 must be avoided. During these xenophobic periods South
Africa has been negatively portrayed in the international press,
but more relevant to South Africa, we have damaged our international relationships.

For many years the Free Market Foundation has called for the
protection of rights of the unemployed and for these people to
be shielded from the rigid labour laws, minimum-wage laws,
and the extensions of bargaining council agreements that result

in job losses. The freedom enshrined in the Constitution states that people should 'not be deprived of freedom arbitrarily or without just cause'.[13] This protection should surely include all forms of freedom, among them the right of all individuals to enter into employment agreements on terms and conditions that are acceptable to them, particularly when there is no other way of securing the 'freedom and security of the person' as undertaken in the Constitution.[14]

It is apparent that no matter how well intentioned South Africa's labour legislation is, it has had significant damaging effects, specifically in terms of job creation. Let us consider some of the job-stoppers created by the Labour Relations Act of 1995. SMEs play a significant role in the economy. 'More than 50% of people in formal jobs in South Africa are employed by SMEs, and more than 60% of new jobs created every year are created by these businesses.'[15] However, these enterprises are finding it increasingly difficult to keep afloat because of the challenges they face due to government legislation.

According to the World Economic Forum's Global Competitiveness Report 2013–2014, South Africa ranks significantly lower than other emerging economies in respect of issues relating to business development and expansion. South Africa ranked 53rd out of 148 countries 'as a result of labour strikes, a struggling education system and government bureaucracy'.[16] South Africa was rated 82 in respect of the number of days required to start a business, 116 in terms of labour market efficiency, 144 for flexibility of wage determination, and 147 for hiring and firing practices. These factors inhibit expansion and growth of SMEs. SMEs often find it impossible to comply with restrictive labour conditions. Government needs to consider ways to limit restrictions on SMEs so that they can continue to be major employers without infringing on good business practice.

Employees may work hard, do what is expected of them, be punctual and show respect for their co-workers' and employer's property. However, employees need to offer an employer more substantial benefits. Quite simply, the business of business is profit. Employees have to price their labour at a level at which their production is worth more than their cost to an employer, and employees must be able to agree in advance that, should they renege on the conditions of their employment, it can be terminated in terms of their employment agreement. According to the current labour laws, unemployed people cannot offer either of these compensating benefits. The law prevents job seekers from contracting with potential employers on terms that are agreeable to both parties, thus preventing them from offering these benefits. These laws that are supposedly imposed for the employees' benefit are effectively keeping people unemployed.

The government has legislated job security, and this has resulted in fewer jobs being available to the unemployed, especially those unemployed whose prospects are already compromised due to age or to lack of skills, education, and experience. This mandated job security discourages employers; they do not want to be tied to workers who don't conform to the expectations in or development of the business.

COSATU would have us believe that a minimum wage would increase economic growth and that the International Monetary Fund's suggestion that labour unions should commit to 'wage restraint' is misguided. These are fallacious notions. Far from being a boost to job creation, the minimum wage is a major deterrent to job creation. If we were to adopt the proposal by COSATU's Patrick Craven that higher wages will bring about higher economic growth by stimulating consumer sales, we'd be in serious trouble. If we take this argument and pass a law that says every worker must be paid R20 000 a month, how many businesses could maintain that expense? How many people would still have jobs? Common sense tells us that a wage at that level would cause massive job losses. It also tells us that at any level, an enforced minimum wage would cause some degree of unemployment. By enforcing a minimum wage, all the government is doing is prohibiting employment and enforcing poverty.

The only solution is to allow for a negotiated wage, an arrangement whereby an employer and an employee agree on a wage that is satisfactory to them both, and only them. Truly engineering a decrease in poverty requires that the freedom enshrined in our Constitution should allow parties the freedom to contract on terms that are agreeable to them alone. Only once this has been achieved will we start to see any meaningful rise in employment. A wage that is lower than what trade unions feel is fair may not be seen in the same way by a frustrated job seeker who simply seeks to get onto the lowest rung of the employment ladder. The current restrictive labour legislation doesn't even allow that first step to be taken, effectively keeping the unemployed poor and unemployed.

Entire sectors of the economy face eradication if labour legislation continues to enforce socialist labour practices in a capitalist economy. The most notable of collapsed sectors is the clothing industry. Newcastle, situated in KwaZulu-Natal 'was the largest garment processing base in South Africa'.[17] It experienced a crippling 60% unemployment rate when its clothing factories were forced to comply with the bargaining council agreements that were extended to non-parties. There was an immediate change in the town's economy as factories were unable to comply with legislation and eventually shut down in solidarity when they were forced to pay fines they could not afford; subsequently huge job losses were reported. This type of sector eradication not only harms industry and results in job losses; it also precludes South Africa from being competitive in international markets. And when an industry sector shuts down, we are forced to import those goods, raising the cost of living.

If the massive rate of unemployment doesn't spur the government to action, then perhaps officials should pay attention to the international critics of our economy. In the Economic Freedom of the World rankings, South Africa slid from 41st in the world in 2000 to 93rd in 2012, predicting lower economic growth.[18] These rankings measure the various factors that determine the level of freedom in the economies of the 152 countries assessed. Overall, South Africa is ranked at 96th in the world on labour regulation. Our scores on the various labour ratings (out of 10) are: hiring regulations and minimum wage 4.43; hiring and firing regulations 1.92; and centralised collective bargaining 3.08. However, COSATU ignores these ratings and disputes the FMF and the International Monetary Fund recommendations that inflexible labour laws contribute to our economic woes.

Vic van Vuuren, South African director of the International Labour Organization (ILO), disputes that South Africa's labour regulations are 'excessively rigid'. He notes: 'When we look at our labour laws and we analyse them and compare them to other best-practice countries, I don't think we have a rigid labour market that is preventing youth employment or employment in general.'[19] What is immediately apparent in Van Vuuren's comment is that he is comparing our labour laws with those of other best-practice countries, namely those in the Organisation for Economic Co-operation and Development (OECD), where 10% unemployment is a crisis. COSATU and the ILO are not comparing apples with apples. Regionally, comparable countries such as Namibia only released their unemployment statistics for the first time in 2013, and Botswana, Nigeria, Zambia and Zimbabwe have not even released unemployment statistics. Looking at other developing countries, it is evident that South Africa's unemployment rate is escalating. When considering comparisons made with similar countries, it would be prudent to bear in mind that all unemployment statistics are problematic in that often the old woman selling a few sweets at the side of the road is considered employed, and people who have given up actively seeking work are not considered in the statistics at all, making the unemployment rate significantly higher than indicated.

UNEMPLOYMENT RATES COMPARED (PERCENTAGES), 2011–2014

SOLID LINE = SOUTH AFRICA (% ON LEFT); DASHED LINE = OTHER COUNTRY NAME (% ON RIGHT)

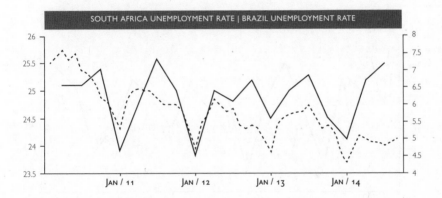

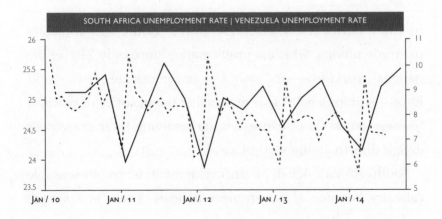

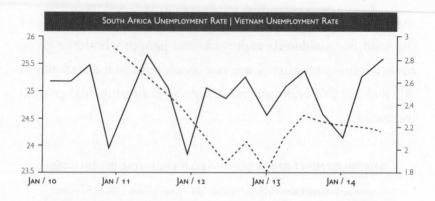

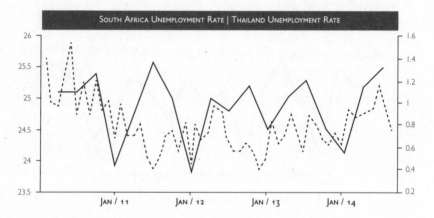

Source: Trading Economics[20]

In South Africa the sole representatives of the workforce are the trade unions, which is problematic, 'since only 24% of the national workforce—and only 15% of the private sector work-force—is unionized'.[21] This means that the majority of workers 'possess no mode of expressing or resolving their grievances except directly in the workplace'.[22]

South Africa's level of unemployment is an inexcusable calamity because of government policies. There is a simple solution. If we remove the rigidities from the labour laws, allow unemployed people to make decisions about their own lives, allow business to hire and fire without fear, and allow voluntary agreements between consenting parties, we will create the millions of jobs our citizens so desperately need. To realise solid and meaningful employment gains, the Department of Labour has to live by its stated vision of 'striving for a labour market which is conducive to investment, economic growth, employment creation and decent work'.[23]

South Africa's current high unemployment rate is similar to that of Hong Kong in the 1960s when Hong Kong was flooded by refugees from China and Vietnam, which led to mass unemployment levels. Jobs were scarce and the British administration in Hong Kong could not do much to help. What they did do was to adopt a policy they called 'positive non-intervention', which meant no strict labour laws, no minimum-wage laws, a low tax rate of 16%, and regulation only for safety, otherwise leaving the economy in the hands of the market. At the time, Hong Kong's per capita gross domestic product (GDP) was 40% of that of the United Kingdom. Twenty years later the per capita GDP was 140% of the UK's, and it is now 150%. Hong Kong has for many decades been first in the world in economic freedom rankings.

Another great example to learn from is Singapore. In 1959 the late Lee Kuan Yew became prime minister of the poor underdeveloped island of Singapore and turned it into the economic powerhouse it is today. Lee Kuan Yew studied law at Cambridge University and practised as a barrister in London for almost 10 years before returning to Singapore and entering politics. His involvement in the British legal system had a great influence on the policies and approach he followed as prime minister of Singapore. He ensured that the legal system functioned properly, that the laws treated everyone equally, and that his government adopted policies that allowed business to flourish. Not surprisingly, international comparisons have found that the Singaporean courts are among the most efficient, and the country ranks highly on the rule-of-law index. Because of these policies, major companies invest in Singapore, a thriving financial services business exists, and foreign direct investment is extremely high for a country with a population of only 5.5 million people, of whom 2.1 million are not citizens but have permanent residence status. Singapore has one of the most free economies in the world. Together with Hong Kong, it is regarded as one of the most competitive economies and among the least corrupt of nations. Singapore has an excellent competitive private/public health care system, and the life expectancy of Singaporeans at birth is 82 years, compared with the 53 years of South Africans. Singapore has a GDP per capita of $60 000 compared with South Africa's $11 000 and an unemployment rate of 2% compared with our unemployment rates of around 25% overall and more than 50% for young people.

South Africa should be learning from these exceptional cases; we should be making economic growth our priority to assist the country to tackle the serious challenges of unemployment, poverty, and inequality.

CHAPTER 6

DISCONTENT AND PROTESTS

Every step of the journey to topple the apartheid regime was marked by citizen protest. With its long history of protests during apartheid, and the most notable post-1994 protests from Harrismith in 2004 to Marikana in 2012, South Africa is regarded as 'the protest capital of the world'.[1] Our history and statute books are populated with Acts and policies that restrict protest, but South Africans have always taken to the street to voice their demands, and, accordingly, section 17 of the Bill of Rights in Chapter 2 of the Constitution gives every South African the democratic right to orderly protest.[2]

The Regulation of Gatherings Act of 1993 states that a gathering is 'a march, picket or parade of 16 people or more taking place in any public space ... [and] is understood as an activity that expresses any form of contestation or is critical towards any person, company or government body ... [and] requires prior notification to the relevant local authority'.[3] A demonstration comprises 15 people or fewer and requires no notification.

It should be noted that notification does not mean requesting permission, since 'no one needs permission to exercise their constitutional right to assemble, picket, march or demonstrate'.[4]

During the first three months of 2014 South Africa experienced 'nearly 3 000 protest actions ... more than 30 a day'— unusually high but not unprecedented. 'The last time South Africa experienced this level of daily public protest was when the United Democratic Front (UDF) and COSATU's ungovernability campaigns and rolling mass action of the late 1980s aimed at bringing the apartheid government to its knees.'[5] Water shortages and electricity disruption are currently widespread due to lack of maintenance and failure to upgrade the ageing infrastructure inherited in 1994. More than two million South Africans have participated in service delivery protests since 2008.[6] According to American civil rights activist Bayard Rustin: 'When an individual is protesting society's refusal to acknowledge his dignity as a human being, his very act of protest confers dignity on him.'[7]

Service delivery protests, whether they take the form of gatherings or demonstrations, continue to feature in every South African province because citizens are dissatisfied with the substandard quality of infrastructure, services, employment prospects, public health, and education; the level of crime; and the rate of reform. Sudden and unofficial strikes proliferate in the agricultural, transport, energy, postal, metal, and mining sectors. Some of these protests have turned violent and have had devastating effects on the protestors, the economy, and the government's international credibility, the most notable of these being the large-scale protests surrounding the Marikana strike near Rustenburg in 2012, which resulted in the death of 44 miners and injuries to many, many more. The violent clashes between police and miners resulted in political infighting in the ruling tripartite alliance, and an investigation into what actually happened has been completed by the Farlam Commission.

Additionally, protestors often feel that the government is not listening to their demands and that they have no alternative but to engage in extreme measures. 'When people protest and burn tyres, and blood is shed, that is when you get a response,' said local activist Pharks Khaiyane. 'When you call a meeting and speak to them [local officials], it's like you're speaking another language. But when you burn tyres, that language is understood.'[8] University of Johannesburg researcher Trevor Ngwane says: 'After 20 years, after the failure to address specific demands, the dissatisfaction is becoming generalized'.[9]

And for good reason, because ironies abound. In any suburban health club, health-conscious people walk around toting bottled mineral water they have bought. If South Africa has the resources to sustain a lucrative bottled water industry, why then in April 2011 did more than 4 000 Ficksburg protestors have to demand access to running water? The community had made written requests to the Ficksburg mayor and the local municipality, urging that attention be given to providing basic amenities, but the mayor and council officials were dismissive of these demands. During the protest Andries Tatane complained about the police firing a water canon at an elderly person, and in response Tatane was struck repeatedly by police batons and rubber bullets. He later died of his wounds. On the day that six policemen appeared in court for Tatane's death, *The Times* newspaper reported that Ficksburg's Mayor Mbothoma Maduna said: '"People say there is no water in this town. What is this?" [he] giggled, reaching into his office fridge for bottles of Valpre mineral water.'[10] The mayor's disdainful and inhumane response highlights the contemptuous attitude of some public officials—some show absolutely no commitment to serious social issues and seem to have only their own selfish interests at heart. Both Tatane's death and the massacre at Marikana are testament to officialdom saying that they don't want to engage on service delivery issues, that they don't care about providing their citizens with basic water services, and that they won't tolerate protest.

Ignoring the anti-Zuma sentiments expressed at many of these protests, Deputy President Cyril Ramaphosa would have us believe that protests are not directed against the ANC-led government in itself but are 'a message that the provision of services in the former townships and informal settlements should be improved'.[11] Researcher Peter Alexander has made a comparative assessment based on the scale of these protests.[12] Writing in the *Mail & Guardian*, he notes: 'As many commentators and activists now accept, service-delivery protests are part of a broader "rebellion of the poor". This rebellion is massive. I have not yet found any other country where there is a similar level of ongoing urban unrest.'[13] The deputy secretary-general of the ANC, Jessie Duarte, proposed various reasons for the protests. She blamed the EFF for precipitating the violence at some protests; she also suggested that some protests were the result of power struggles between ANC branches and leaders of the South African National Civic Organisation (SANCO), itself an ANC structure. Yet other analysts have attributed the protests to bored, unemployed youths and criminal-minded community members.

While there are probably elements of truth in all these scenarios, what I regard as the foundation of these protests is deep-rooted anger—the anger of more than 20 years looking for release. People are desperately angry that they have no jobs, that they cannot afford to feed or house themselves and their families, that they have to live in miserable environments lacking basic amenities, and that they have a deep sense of despair at not being heard, especially by corrupt local, provincial, and national authorities. All these feelings wind up reduced to a simmering discontent, and the government, at its peril, undermines the foundation of this discontent.

In September 2013 eTV invited me to attend and judge its 'Mumbai MBA in a Day' programme in India. On location in Mumbai I witnessed poverty on an unimaginable scale. I spent hours walking through the slums of Mumbai. Anyone who has seen the movie or read the book *Slumdog Millionaire* will have some understanding of the conditions in the Mumbai slums. Although I walked through the Indian city at all hours of the day and night, at no stage did I feel threatened, intimidated or insecure in the same way that I would have had I been in a South African city. Comparing Mumbai with our slum areas is like comparing Alexandra with Sandton—the poverty in Mumbai is diabolical, and yet these grossly and indecently marginalised people are entrepreneurs, people who know they have nobody but themselves to look out for them. The astounding reality is that the Indian poor have given up relying on the government for support. Their survival instinct is so well honed that even though it is admirable, it is deeply shaming to humanity. I couldn't help wondering how long it would take before this scenario is a reality in South Africa.

Over its first two decades in power the ANC government has implemented five major economic policies: the Reconstruction and Development Programme (RDP) in 1994; the Growth, Employment and Redistribution (GEAR) strategy in 1996; the Accelerated and Shared Growth Initiative—South Africa (ASGISA) in 2005; the New Growth Path (NGP) in 2010; and the National Development Plan (NDP) in 2013.

The RDP was the ANC's poster child for the 1994 elections, outlining five major policy programmes: to 'create a strong, dynamic and balanced economy; [develop] human resource capacity of all South Africans; ensure that no one suffers racial or gender discrimination in hiring, promotion or training situations; develop a prosperous, balanced regional economy in Southern Africa; and democratise the state and society' in the hope that this would result in 'the final eradication of apartheid and the building of a democratic, non-racial and non-sexist future'.[14] If we look at the achievements under the RDP, we find that 1.1 million cheap houses were built, housing five million people. However, these houses were provided at great expense to the country and the communities; RDP officials were accused of corruption and fund mismanagement, and contractors built substandard homes that cost the government millions to repair. Communities erupted in violence when they realised that it wasn't as easy as putting your name down to receive a house.

Although Minister of Water Affairs Kader Asmal stated at the time that the RDP had provided 2.5 million people with access to safe water and 4.9 million people with piped clean water, the water projects were beleaguered by serious engineering faults and bureaucratic bungling, which ironically led to more people relying on natural water resources during the period 1995 to 1999.[15] In an attempt to calm irate citizens, the government announced a major policy shift in 2000 to provide households with 6 000 litres of free water per month. How sustainable an economic policy was this, and where was the money going to come from to fund this handout?

In terms of land reform, the RDP managed to resettle families on only 1% of the original target of 300 000 km² of land. Probably the RDP's most alarming let-down was that the government removed agricultural subsidies, an action whereby more than half of the workers on commercial farms lost their jobs—reducing the commercial farming workforce from 1.4 million to 637 000 people. Thus the RDP actually exacerbated unemployment.[16]

Between 1994 and 1998 hundreds of new clinics provided primary health care to five million people, but standards at South African medical facilities declined miserably. Between 1995 and 1998 South Africans' life expectancy decreased from 64.1 years to 53.2 years, and AIDS patients occupied 40% of public hospital beds. Professor Tom Lodge notes that, in 1994, 950 000 Sowetan patients were attended to by 800 nurses, and, in 2000, 2 million patients were attended to by only 500 nurses, putting untenable pressure on the medical fraternity.[17] This scenario is hardly one of a public health system undergoing positive change; instead it illuminates a serious crisis. It is apparent that the RDP failed because it did not implement policies successfully, because unskilled project and programme managers were employed, and because the government tried to do things on the cheap by relying on existing revenues instead of increasing the tax base.

When the government realised that the RDP was failing and that resources needed to be aligned to social needs, they introduced GEAR to fuel economic growth. Whereas the RDP had focused on social transformation, GEAR focused on getting the financing right to lower inflation, reduce fiscal deficits, maintain a stable exchange rate, relax capital flows, and decrease barriers to trade.[18] GEAR's major drive was to privatise and restructure government-owned enterprises, such as Telkom, Transnet, Denel, and Eskom. We have only to look at Eskom to see how disastrous that has been. The extreme pressure brought to bear on an underfunded corporation with an ailing infrastructure was unsustainable, and we have seen the spectacular fallout whereby we now find ourselves in a situation of limited access to electricity. It is unreasonable to expect corporate and industrial South Africa to function when services are disrupted to this extent. During the GEAR period, job creation and private investment declined, the distribution of wealth was disappointing, and of course poverty was not reduced.

In 2005 the government introduced ASGISA, realising that unalleviated poverty was a huge bugbear and that social issues needed to be the focus of economic policy. However, critics warned that no economic policy would succeed unless the government moved sharply to address the very real issues of corruption, labour costs, high tax rates, and crime.

After President Thabo Mbeki was unceremoniously ousted from office, President Jacob Zuma announced the NGP in 2010. The NGP was an upgraded ASGISA, zooming in on accelerating the economy to reduce poverty and to create the levels of employment that the ANC had been promising since 1994. Increased government intervention has proven to be harmful to South Africa's economic freedom. It is internationally accepted that prosperity can exist only if freedom exists. Government's BEE and minimum-wage legislation did not increase employment, because only liberalised, capitalist economies can stimulate job creation. The only way of ensuring job creation and improved working conditions is to increase the demand for labour in order to create conditions that promote the desire to hire more employees.

A major failure of the NGP has been policy regarding

education and training. ASGISA proposed that the government actively train state employees so that the government could realise its social objectives, namely, to raise standards of living, create new jobs, and sustain improved economic growth. This is exactly what the National Party did during apartheid: it trained as artisans the white workers who worked in the state-owned enterprises. But can the government really wear two hats? Can it be the government and the country's employer? I doubt it. Bureaucrats possess neither the experience nor the background to train a competent workforce. Where would they get the knowledge to bring the right type of employee to market? In reality, most training occurs at the coalface; it is in the company offices or on the shop floor that people are made employment-ready. For the government to press skills training onto private employers is ludicrous. As a businessman, I know that employers will train workers only if they consider it to be profitable. It is disingenuous on the part of government to use its political power to brandish the stick and insist that employers conduct training irrespective of the cost to business.

In 2013 the government introduced the NDP 2030, which is the blueprint for the ANC's future economic and socio-economic development strategy. Its focus is on SMEs creating almost 10 million jobs. At the very outset this is an unrealistic assumption. Affirmative action and limiting labour legislation already enacted have not encouraged the establishment of the SMEs that needed to be created to facilitate this job growth. The government simply has to understand that only a liberalised economy

UNEMPLOYMENT STATISTICS IN THE BRICS COUNTRIES		
COUNTRY	UNEMPLOYMENT	DATE OF DATA
Brazil	6.2%	March 2015
Russia	5.9%	March 2015
India	4.9%	December 2013
China	4.1%	February 2015
South Africa	24.3%	November 2014

Source: http://www.tradingeconomics.com/country-list/unemployment-rate

can foster new business establishment. Until it recognises this, there is no hope of achieving any of its other economic goals.

Thus it is evident that South Africa's economic policies, in particular those since the beginning of majority rule in 1994, are solely responsible for the government's failure to provide jobs for millions of our fellow South Africans, resulting in one of the highest unemployment rates in the developing world.

For more than 20 years the government has been showcasing its micro-economic achievements. Indeed, the Twenty Year Review states: 'In essence ... [the government] adopted fiscal and monetary policies aimed at maintaining economic stability, while seeking to bring about economic transformation and increase productivity through micro-economic interventions.'[19] It seems that the ruling party does not understand the significance of macro-economic policy, or has lost sight of it, and instead focuses on micro-economic success stories as evidence of successes. According to the government's micro-economic reform strategy, 'government controls the following four input sectors: transport, energy, water and telecommunications, and can therefore ensure that these sectors are cost competitive, efficient and accessible'.[20] This is clearly not the case, since South Africa has witnessed and continues to experience severe water and electricity shortages, and the post office has suffered an extended and debilitating strike. Protests are taking place against every one of these sectors, indicating that the ANC government is definitely not delivering services that are competitive, efficient, or accessible.

The government, through micro-economic initiatives, is simply not capable of stimulating the economy and providing the type of environment necessary to create the employment needed in this country. To stimulate business and real growth, the government needs to focus on the macro-economic environment. I'm a businessman, and I know that business people want security of tenure in which to operate. We need political stability, and the assurance that our investments will not be confiscated or appropriated by the government and that our business efforts will not be strangled by legislation. Business owners want an economic framework that facilitates trade and has favourable import tariffs, preferential trade agreements, and sound banking regulations. Admittedly our banking sector is a shining example of what we can achieve; our biggest banks are efficient technology innovators and trade facilitators. Additionally, business requires infrastructural development

COMPOSITION OF GDP BY MAJOR INDUSTRIES, 1994 AND 2012

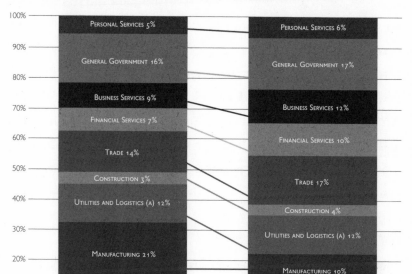

Source: Open Government Partnership in the Twenty Year Review, p. 88

from the government—business needs uninterrupted power and water service and the transportation and logistics to move goods around; business requires efficient billing, efficient communication and cellular data, but most important, business needs a skilled labour force that is productive and efficient. These are the things that make up an environment in which business can flourish. Business does not need over-legislation; all over-legislation does is protect big monopolies. Over-regulation doesn't encourage entrepreneurship; it creates too many barriers to entry. Only when the government provides

AGRICULTURE AS A PERCENTAGE OF GDP, 1996–2012

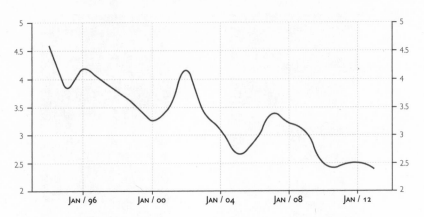

Source: Trading Economics, Agriculture—Value added (% of GDP) in South Africa 1994–2014[23]

what the economy, via business, really needs, will we see fewer protests from the unemployed, the under-served and the poor, because when business is able to operate unimpeded, employment increases.

If we consider the composition of the GDP by major industries, it is immediately apparent in which sectors the government is failing the country, namely in manufacturing and agriculture. These two sectors are vital to economic performance. The former provides labour and export opportunities, and the latter provides food, labour, and export opportunities. President Mbeki's aim was to increase manufacturing, but indicators are that manufacturing's contribution to the GDP decreased by a substantial 11% over the 18-year period reflected.

The increased job creation that the government insists has occurred, and a weaker rand, should have resulted in an increase in manufacturing; that this has not happened is an indicator

SOUTH AFRICA'S BALANCE OF TRADE, 1996–2012 (ZAR MILLION)

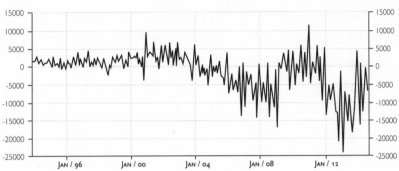

Source: Trading Economics, South African Revenue Service

that there is something seriously wrong in what the government is doing. The fact is that South Africa is not globally competitive; we probably aren't sufficiently competitive in areas such as productivity, and therefore we cannot compete globally even though we have so-called low wages that the unions are constantly seeking to increase.

The same principles can be applied to agriculture and mining. Both sectors employ significant numbers of people, and agriculture's contribution to the GDP continues to slide.

Mining has also slumped significantly, and we have reached the stage where 'mining products, as a percentage of total exports, [have] decreased from 57.3% (in value terms) in 1994 to 49.1% in 2012'.[21]

The increase in trade has been largely a one-way situation, and South Africa is importing more than we ever used to do. Our balance of trade is negative and has been for the past decade (see balance of trade graph above); we are importing far more than we are exporting.[22] What measures is the government implementing in an attempt to counter this situation? At one stage the Reserve Bank and the Minister of Finance made a concerted effort to manage this situation actively, but now we appear to have thrown in the towel. Ultimately, if we continue this trend, we are going to manufacture less and import more, create fewer jobs, provide less stimulus to start new businesses, and continue to weaken the rand, which will create more inflation, which in turn will result in unions demanding higher wages, making the South African business sector even less competitive. A disaster.

More government jobs are being created, but all that this has resulted in is a bloated civil service that is highly inefficient. There are more people in government doing less. The inefficiency in some departments has reached extreme proportions, and it costs the South African taxpayer more to fund these inefficiencies, which is not a healthy situation. The result of this inefficiency is service boycotts around the country. There is not a single province that hasn't experienced these boycotts.

If there is any consolation, it is that we can look at other countries and see that we are not alone in this kind of mess. But the other instances also show that matters have not ended well for those countries. Greece is a notable example, where multiple government jobs for life held by a single person are de rigueur, much like our ghost workers here. The syndrome has been and continues to be a disastrous drain on public funds. The next stages in this unsustainable situation are a deficit in the budget, more borrowings, and ultimately the possibility of a debt default, such as in Argentina.

The South African Institute of Race Relations succinctly sums up the situation, stating that 'the sluggish economic growth is not paralleled by job creation and many people are unable to be absorbed into private sectors while increasing dependency on the state. In this regard, better service delivery is viewed as not an answer but increasing private sector employment is seen a[s] key to defusing popular anger against the state.'[24]

The ongoing service delivery protests are a significant challenge in South Africa. The government's failure to respond to community issues increases frustration and anger and is confirmation that the government has failed to meet the most basic needs of its citizens.

In addition to the social and economic issues that South Africans are protesting against, what could be the psychological reason that motivates protest? According to James C Davies in his article, Toward a theory of revolution, there is a fear that 'ground gained over a long period of time will be quickly lost. This fear does not generate if there is continued opportunity to satisfy continually emerging needs; it generates when the existing government suppresses or is blamed for suppressing such opportunity.'[25] This supposition may well be aligned with black South African thought in that many black people feel that what they fought for long and hard no longer looks as though it's going to happen and that the government can no longer deliver on its promises.

TOP THREE REASONS FOR PROTESTS

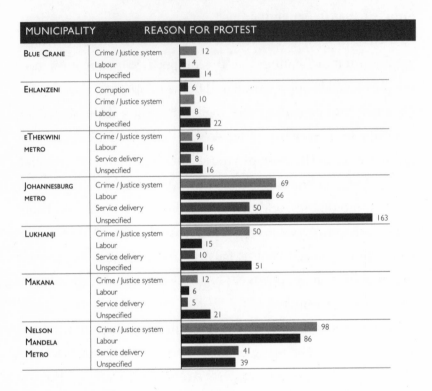

MUNICIPALITY	REASON FOR PROTEST	
Blue Crane	Crime / Justice system	12
	Labour	4
	Unspecified	14
Ehlanzeni	Corruption	6
	Crime / Justice system	10
	Labour	8
	Unspecified	22
eThekwini Metro	Crime / Justice system	9
	Labour	16
	Service delivery	8
	Unspecified	16
Johannesburg Metro	Crime / Justice system	69
	Labour	66
	Service delivery	50
	Unspecified	163
Lukhanji	Crime / Justice system	50
	Labour	15
	Service delivery	10
	Unspecified	51
Makana	Crime / Justice system	12
	Labour	6
	Service delivery	5
	Unspecified	21
Nelson Mandela Metro	Crime / Justice system	98
	Labour	86
	Service delivery	41
	Unspecified	39

Source: *Mail & Guardian* [26]

Note that in a 2014 *Mail & Guardian* tally of reasons for protests, labour—that is, unemployment—was routinely cited among the top three reasons. People expect to be able to find decent work at decent wages.

Davies takes this idea a step further: 'Revolutions are most likely to occur when a prolonged period of objective economic and social development is followed by a short period of sharp reversal. People then subjectively fear that ground gained with great effort will be quite lost; their mood becomes revolutionary.'[27] This is evident in the mood of South African protestors.

According to Karl Marx: 'A noticeable increase in wages

presupposes a rapid growth of productive capital. The rapid growth of productive capital brings about an equally rapid growth of wealth, luxury, social wants, social enjoyments. Thus, although the enjoyments of the workers have risen, the social satisfaction that they give has fallen in comparison with the increased enjoyments of the capitalist, which are inaccessible to the worker, in comparison with the state of development of society in general.'[28]

We only have to look at the unprecedented rise in the popularity of the EFF to realise that this is indeed the case in South Africa. The ANC refuses to acknowledge the discontent simmering on the social landscape. Unless the ANC meets the economic demands on which the protestors are insisting, it faces the danger of social and political revolution, a danger that could be eliminated by listening to its people.

CHAPTER 7

CORRUPTION AND CIVIC RESPONSIBILITY

South Africa's continuing problems and challenges can be overwhelming at times. The effects of crime, lack of service delivery, and unemployment can be crushing to even the most positive of patriots, and political fatigue may set in. My vision for South Africa is a broad and hopeful one, and to keep my focus on that vision, I cannot dwell on the country's immediate problems. I would never have succeeded in business if I had allowed existing conditions to discourage me. The most overwhelming experience in my professional career was when my business burned down. I knew as I stood and watched the building turn to ashes that I had to rise above the crisis. I had employees counting on me to continue the business, I had a family to support, and I knew that falling to pieces was not an option. Likewise, I will not stand by and watch the country I so deeply love disintegrate.

The most useful way I have found to combat and avoid despair has been to immerse myself in civic pursuits that remind me there are individuals and organisations seeking to develop South Africa by being proactive. I have always tried to assimilate myself into situations and organisations that uphold my ideals and where I feel I will be best placed to contribute to society. Being South African means playing a role in our beautiful country.

The first civic responsibility programme I was involved in was the voting education effort I sponsored in the 1994 election. Other such involvements followed, and I served as chair of the Institute of Directors in Southern Africa from June 2008 to June 2011. Business has always been my first priority, and the institute's vision that 'directors and others charged with governance duties in all sectors are empowered to discharge these duties effectively' has resonated with me because I believe strong directorship and leadership ultimately lead to strong businesses that will bring about an improved South Africa for all South Africans.[1]

In 2004 I was awarded the Free Market Award by the Free Market Foundation for 'exceptional contribution to the cause of economic freedom'. I had been a member of the foundation for many years, but I became a member of the board in 2011 to start actively promoting capitalism and ethical leadership. The FMF has strong roots in the formation of our democracy, and it was their inclination towards freedom and the promotion of free markets that particularly appealed to me, as an avowed capitalist.

Committed individuals who sought to steer the country on a

path that would lead it to uphold the values of sound political and economic management established the FMF in 1977. Leon Louw, Eustace Davie, Terry Markman, and Temba Nolutshungu, and many more fellow South Africans are committed men and women whom this country is fortunate to have among its citizens. Dr Sam Motsuenyane, during his tenure as president of the National African Federated Chamber of Commerce and Industry, also served as president of the FMF during the dark days of our country's history. The National Party government regarded the FMF as another communist organisation to challenge the plight and advance the cause of black people, and some members of the current government consider the FMF a neo-liberal organisation bent on advancing the exploitation of the black masses. Most of the FMF's critics have never taken the time to investigate its credentials or community involvement.

In late 2011, I watched a television news item about Julius Malema, at the time the firebrand ANC Youth League president, holding what the ANCYL referred to as an economic freedom march. Their definition of economic freedom was for the government to play a leading role in the economy, including the nationalisation of mines and banks and the expropriation of land. The willing-buyer/willing-seller principle agreed upon during the negotiation process was deemed not to be working; hence the ANCYL believed that the government needed to expropriate the land without compensation.

The march set out from the Chamber of Mines' offices in central Johannesburg, proceeded to the Johannesburg Stock

Exchange in Sandton, and eventually ended at the Union Buildings in Pretoria. According to media reports, the march attracted roughly 15 000 people, mainly unemployed and marginalised South Africans. Minister Thulas Nxesi received the memorandum on behalf of the president and expressed his agreement with Malema's interpretation of economic freedom. After witnessing the destruction of the Zimbabwean economy by such policies, I found myself unable to sit back and do nothing. I have always believed in a free-market economy. My interpretation of economic freedom is the right to sell and buy labour, goods, and services at a price agreed upon by the contractors, without government involvement. With all the other problems being experienced in the country as a result of poor management and rampant corruption, I was surprised to hear the minister support the measures promoted by the Youth League. That incident was a defining moment for me, a call to do something to save our country from economic collapse. I felt I needed to use my privileged position and status to act. Since I regarded myself as a non-political person, the challenge was how would I intervene?

In a state of confusion and despair, I considered approaching the Free Market Foundation for advice. I invited FMF Executive Director Leon Louw to lunch and shared my frustration and fears about the potential economic direction that our country seemed likely adopt. Leon is what one might call a true son of the soil; a South African who is committed to the principles of free markets and the rule of law. As an ordinary member of the

FMF over many years, I had regularly received newsletters and invitations to FMF events, which promote and educate members about free markets. Over lunch I asked, 'Leon, why are you communicating these ideals to me? You are preaching to the converted.' I asked him why the foundation wasn't engaging with the 15 000 people who followed Malema on the so-called economic freedom march. I was disappointed to learn that the foundation did not have the necessary resources or capacity to reach this important audience in our country.

This situation inspired me to engage the foundation as to how I could be involved in reaching a wider audience. I approached the FMF Executive Committee and indicated that I was prepared to work with the foundation to explore how I could be of assistance to spread its message to the less-privileged members of South African society. In due course I was appointed to the board, and I recruited other like-minded fellow South Africans to join the board with the primary goal of raising the funds that would allow the FMF to reach this wider audience and thus have a more significant influence on national policy decisions. This decision was motivated by my concern about the crisis in South Africa. I believed that the FMF was the only organisation with the necessary knowledge and ability to persuade government to choose economic freedom, and I did not want to be looking back in years to come knowing I had done nothing.

The FMF is an honourable organisation that promotes the exact policies we need to make South Africa great. Its aim is 'to foster an open society, the rule of law, personal liberty, and economic and press freedom as fundamental components of its advocacy of human rights and democracy based on classical liberal principles'.[2] It sounds to me like a great blueprint for a country. The FMF encourages sound economic policies and sensible laws that will lead to growth, jobs, prosperity, and justice for all South Africans. As I have stated several times, we need to have the right rules in place for all South Africans to enjoy a prosperous future.

The idea of an open society was originally proposed in 1932 by French philosopher Henri Bergson, and was developed in the early 1940s by British philosopher Karl Popper, who stated that 'if we wish to remain human, then there is only one way, the way into the open society … into the unknown, the uncertain and insecure'.[3] He defined an open society as one 'in which individuals are confronted with personal decisions' rather than a 'magical or tribal or collectivist society'.[4] Popper's notion that only democracy can provide an institutional mechanism for reform and leadership without the need for bloodshed or a revolution was indeed the case in South Africa's transition. Political freedom, human rights, critical knowledge and thinking, cultural and religious pluralism, and freedom of thought are fundamental characteristics of an open society and are certainly no different from what our Constitution guarantees. The FMF's promotion of an open society is wholly supportive of our Constitution.

Good governance is simply upholding the rule of law. According to the World Justice Project, the rule of law is defined as 'a rules-based system in which the following four universal principles are upheld:

☐ The government and its officials and agents are account-able under the law.

☐ The laws are clear, publicized, stable and fair, and pro-tect fundamental human rights, including the security of persons and property.

☐ The process by which laws are enacted, administered, and enforced is accessible, fair and efficient.

☐ Access to justice is provided by competent, independent, and ethical adjudicators, attorneys or representatives, and judicial officers who are of sufficient number, have adequate resources, and reflect the makeup of the com-munities they serve.'[5]

If we consider governance and events in South Africa since 1994 in the light of these principles, can we say in all good conscience that the rule of law is being upheld? South Africa suffers from cronyism and corruption at the highest level of government. In 2013 Public Protector Thuli Madonsela told Parliament: 'Corruption in this country has reached crisis proportions, there is no two ways about it.'[6] The executive director of Corruption Watch, David Lewis, says: 'The Gupta wedding saga and ongoing fiasco surrounding the President's private Nkandla residence are indicators in the past year of impunity in oper-ation.'[7] Hamadziripi Tamukamoyo of the Governance, Crime and Justice Division at the Institute for Security Studies says: 'It is not merely that perceptions of corruption worsening have increased; there is hard evidence that actual levels of corruption have increased.'[8] Based on parliamentary documents and data from the Public Service Commission that found that, in the 2011–2012 financial year, public sector fraud and malfeasance cost taxpayers close to R1 billion—an increase from a loss of R130.6 million in the 2006–2007 financial year—Tamukamoyo attributes corruption worsening in South Africa to the lack of accountability that seems to protect perpetrators.[9]

In spite of commissions of inquiry into cases of corruption, it would appear that certain highly placed individuals are evading inquiry, and in certain cases evading prosecution, flouting the rule of law. When did the rot set in? When President Zuma had a criminal case against him dropped because it wouldn't do for the state president to be seen facing criminal charges? When he allowed his Gupta friends to use a national key point airport to land their wedding guests and refused to be accountable? When taxpayers paid for his R246 million upgrade to his private residence? What kind of precedent does that behaviour set? If the president won't adhere to the rule of law, why should anyone else? Moeletsi Mbeki, brother of former president Thabo Mbeki, says: 'There is something very wrong with South Africa, in particular with how the political elite are managing the country.' He refers to many other black politicians as 'architects of poverty' whose 'main objective is to maximize their own consumption and the consumption of those who keep them in power.'[10]

It is thus imperative that organisations such as the FMF, and indeed individuals, continue to insist that the rule of law be adhered to if we are to have any hope of stamping out the rampant corruption that is degrading South Africa in every way.

Cronyism is a cancer that is eliminating fair access to jobs. The ANC has adhered to a policy of cadre deployment and political support for those loyal to the party. The auditor-general disclosed that 'only 5% of municipalities received clean audits for 2010/2011. No metros received clean audits and 13% of municipalities didn't even bother to give their financial statements in on time.'[11]

Of course cronyism exists internationally, and 'Silvio Berlusconi's Italy is an obvious example of how political cronyism can destroy an economy'.[12] David Henderson, a research fellow at the Hoover Institution and editor of *The Fortune Encyclopedia of Economics*, observes: 'Cronyism isn't a zero-sum game that takes from some and gives to others; it's negative-sum. The losses to the losers substantially outweigh the gains to the usually less numerous winners. That's something both sides of the political aisle should be able to agree on. The solution to cronyism is not more politicians meddling in private business. It's the opposite: Let the free market do its job and level the playing field.'[13] This is exactly what the FMF supports.

Many people believe that public policy helps order society. The FMF believes that property rights are fundamental to maintaining a healthy society. Property rights solve problems that public policy cannot solve. Let's consider how this could be. Should businesses implement a minimum wage? Should schools in certain areas adopt a specific language of instruction? Should I be able to roast a cow in my back yard? The first two questions involve public policy; the last one involves behaviour in my home and is a private policy. What is important in these examples is that in the first two questions, the government makes the decisions, but in the last question, I make the decision. But let's say you don't find my roasting a cow acceptable and you decide not to visit me. By doing so, you make a trade-off; you choose not to enjoy my company because you find my cow roasting distasteful. How I choose to use my back yard is not a concern of public policy; it's my back yard, so I get to choose. However, if you enjoy my company, you may respect my property rights and choose to visit me.

And therein lies the importance of my questions. If you respect my property rights, then the other two questions aren't public policy problems either. Should a business implement a minimum wage? The government says it should, and the business owner says it shouldn't. Business owners are aware that by not implementing a minimum wage, they will be able to employ more workers, increase productivity, and accrue better base-line profits. They also know that if they do implement a minimum wage, they have to tailor production according to its cost. They may choose to ignore or adhere to the public policy, but they will do so in ways that maximise their income. We can't ignore their employees, so it's possible that the business owners will either pay the minimum wage to keep their

workers satisfied or employ fewer people to adhere to the legislation. Basically, the minimum wage should be a private issue;
the only people making the decision should be the owner and
the employees who choose to accept the wage. But it is a public
policy problem because the government has made it one. I'm a
vociferous defender of property rights, and I believe that public
policies are very often extreme violations of people's property
rights. If individuals could exercise their property rights, the
conflict around public policy would disappear. As Henderson
says, problems that appear to be public policy problems are
only so 'because the government has chosen to make them so.
Private property solves people's problems every day.'[14]

Although the Constitution guarantees a dispensation based
on free enterprise, enterprise is being strangled by obstructive
laws and regulations, as I have shown; and the Constitution
and the rule of law are being flouted by the very people who
should be upholding them. The FMF's task is to propose better ways of doing things and turning to the courts for relief,
as we are doing with the labour law challenge, challenging the
aspects of governance that create unemployment and destroy
entrepreneurship and small business.

The FMF seeks to persuade the policy-makers to sweep away
the barriers that prevent people from getting jobs and to create
conditions that will allow people to take responsibility for their
own lives. The current untenable situation that keeps more than
eight million people unemployed simply has to be eradicated.
I have a vision for South Africa. I envisage no labour shortage,

employers offering jobs to every single person who wants to work and get ahead, and a country where young people are encouraged to be diligent students and improve their skills so that they are employable or able to start their own businesses. I especially envisage youth who believe there are no limits to success.

South Africa desperately needs entrepreneurs, and we need people who advance strategies to provide the people around us with what they need and want. Entrepreneurs do things differently from the way they have previously been done and use resources differently from the way they have earlier been used. It isn't always easy to identify opportunities, but they are there for the taking. Unemployed people shouldn't wait for jobs to come to them; they should think about how they can benefit themselves while serving others. That is what free-market capitalism is all about. When I was a youngster, I didn't have a job, and there were minimal opportunities in the apartheid-created homeland at Hammanskraal, which had little to no access to transport or opportunities and where Bantu education provided scant skills. But I did have good social skills. I used these social skills as a 'knoxman' in illegal dice games, and I managed to make good money out of gambling. After being employed at Spar and Motani furnishers, I started working for myself and sold linen and crockery and cutlery out of the boot of my car, taking products to my clients and convincing them that they needed a new bedroom set or fine new cups and saucers (see Black Like You for more about linen and dice games). I had saved for the car while working for others, and I bought it without even knowing how to drive, because I was convinced that mobility would allow me to work independently and advance me up the ladder towards my goals. It may take small, incremental steps to reach goals, but every journey starts with that first step.

In addition to working to assist the unemployed, the FMF is cooperating with local authorities to give council housing tenants freehold title to their houses. The FMF embarked on this project in the Ngwathe municipal area in the Free State by identifying a community and approaching the local authorities and sponsors to partner with the FMF to transfer ownership of the council houses to the tenants. It has been rewarding to see many families become homeowners, and while the FMF continues to raise finance for the conveyancing costs related to transfer, it is their hope that as a result of seeing this example, many more families will become homeowners—families that heretofore had no hope of owning their homes. Home ownership provides people with real, secure property rights, protected by the Constitution, and the true freedom that has been denied to them for so long. It also provides a foundation on which the homeowners can build their communities and improve their lives; home ownership underpins wealth building.

The FMF has embarked on several other national community projects to improve the lives of South Africans. It has urged government to free up the electricity supply system so that private generating companies can provide the electricity the country so desperately needs. ANC Secretary-General Gwede Mantashe has come out in defence of private electricity supply companies, and we need only look at the Scandinavian countries and Australia to see that competition is driving the price of electricity down and releasing government from the burden of supplying this amenity. We have load-shedding and rolling blackouts, and the disruptions to our power supply are damaging to the economy. How can a company operate effectively without electricity? In a free-market economy Eskom would allow competition, and consumers would have a choice of suppliers. Why not allow entrepreneurs, both domestic and corporate, to generate their own electricity and sell off their excess? This type of entrepreneurial suppression represses innovation and eliminates solutions that would build our country.

Having grown up largely without role models, I know how important it is to inspire a nation that is sorely in need of role models. To this end the FMF identifies unique individuals who inspire others in a particular sector, nationally and internationally, and honours them with Luminary Awards. It is important to celebrate people who have overcome adversity or are determined to make a difference in the lives of others through their achievements. Illuminating the achievements of such individuals has a positive influence on people who feel frustrated or uncertain of what life has to offer them.

During my tenure as chairman of the foundation, I was privileged to be involved in recognising and making awards to some of the outstanding recipients of the Luminary Awards. Our first recipient was Dr Yuri Maltsev, an economics professor at Carthage College, Wisconsin, in the United States. Dr Maltsev was given the award for his tireless dedication to upholding liberty and for the inspiration he brings to the people whose lives he touches. A defector to the United States in the late 1980s, he is a labour economist and was one of the advisors to the Mikhail Gorbachev government.

Our second recipient was an outstanding South African, the Most Reverend Archbishop Dr Thabo Makgoba. Dr Makgoba was acknowledged for his lifelong dedication to all the people of South Africa and for ceaselessly demonstrating the highest level of integrity. The third award went to Dr Pauline Dixon, a director of research at the EG West Centre at Newcastle University. Dr Dixon was acknowledged for her dedication to researching and tirelessly promoting practical solutions to schooling challenges and educational entrepreneurship in low-income communities.

The fourth award went to the remarkable South African businessman, Dr Sam Motsuenyane, for outstanding individual enterprise excellence and leadership, consistently demonstrated over many decades in overcoming adversity and inspiring the people of South Africa. Our fifth award was bestowed on one of the finest legal minds in South Africa, Advocate George Bizos, for dedicating his entire life to fighting injustice and for the promotion of civil liberties.

Subsequent to my resignation as chairman of the foundation,

although I still remained as a full member, a further two outstanding South Africans were recognised with awards. The sixth and seventh awards went to outstanding businessmen Dr Richard Maponya and Raymond Ackerman, respectively.

Free-market principles are sound values on which to establish stability and prosperity in South Africa. The fact that I resigned as chair of the FMF does not in any way attest to my being unsupportive of the foundation and its noble aspirations; I left only because I was joining the Democratic Alliance as a card-carrying member, and I did not want the FMF labelled as a DA front by people opposed to my move. The FMF has always operated on the principle of non-partisanship and must be protected to hold such a position. However, I remain a member of the FMF and lend it my full support, especially in terms of the FMF labour challenge, which is discussed in the next chapter.

CHAPTER 8

LABOUR LAWS ARE KEY

South Africa has numerous inflexibilities in its current labour laws, but as a capitalist and as someone concerned with the plight and rights of fellow South African owners of small and medium enterprises, I propose that the labour provision at the root of unemployment in the country is section 32(2) of the Labour Relations Act 66 of 1995. It reads as follows: 'Within 60 days of receiving the request, the Minister *must* extend the collective agreement, as requested, by publishing a notice in the *Government Gazette* declaring that, from a specified date and for a specified period, the collective agreement will be binding on the non-parties specified in the notice.'[1]

A bargaining council is a sector-specific organisation that facilitates negotiations on working conditions and wages between unified employees (usually trade unions) and employers. In its current form, section 32(2) of the Labour Relations Act determines that the Minister of Labour 'must' extend the bargaining councils' agreed conditions to all employers and employees in the relevant sector. This means that the minister extends the wage and working conditions agreements, often reached by a minority of employers in an industry, to non-parties to the negotiations. It is unconstitutional for the minister to be compelled to extend these agreements to non-parties, and it is undemocratic to compel SME owners to abide by agreements in which they did not participate. As the International Monetary Fund notes in its 2005 Country Report: 'Collective bargaining, through bargaining councils, dominates in many sectors. The bargaining system is relatively centralized.'[2]

In 1980 I rebelled against the apartheid laws that denied us the freedom to make our own decisions about our own lives; apartheid enforced policies that stopped people from achieving their true social, economic, and political potential. At the age of 20, I abandoned my university studies, rejecting the apartheid political and educational system. I wanted to help to bring about political freedom for our country, but my intention to join Umkhonto we Sizwe was thwarted because I did not have the right political contacts to get me out of the country for training to return and cause havoc. I was an angry young man determined to change the course of this system I regarded as evil. The only viable option I could see at the time was military training. I had no other rights as a South African to challenge the apartheid regime. Their language was force.

Mass unemployment is unnatural. It doesn't just happen without a cause. And mass unemployment is doing significant harm to the country's economy. According to the World Economic

Forum's Global Risks 2014 report, 52% of South African youths are unemployed, and South Africa has the third-highest unemployment rate in the world for people aged 15 to 24.[3] Armenia has the highest at 57% and Macedonia the second highest at 54%.[4] Unemployed youths without a sufficient education, or without skills, need to be able to negotiate terms of employment with a prospective employer. Section 32(2) of the Labour Relations Act currently prevents SMEs from employing these unskilled workers, so they remain unemployed as a result of the law supposedly enacted for their benefit.

This situation has to change if South Africa is to decrease its current unemployment rate from 26% to 5%, so that we can be the economic powerhouse we should be.[5] The extension of these bargaining council agreements serves to limit job creation, leads to higher prices, and ultimately creates an uncompetitive economy. It completely excludes and dismisses the small employers and employees, who typically have no voice in these agreements, and who cannot afford to conform to the bargaining council agreements reached by big business and trade unions. Bargaining council agreements are against the spirit of the Constitution that ensures every South African's freedom to work.

Freedom is enshrined in our Constitution, and it is manifested in different forms. We South Africans should have the freedom to decide for ourselves what type of jobs we want to do, how much we are prepared to work for, and under what conditions we are prepared to work. We should have the freedom to make our own decisions about our own lives. Constitutional freedom is freedom that is extended to everyone and is the one accessible right for even very poor and unemployed people. They have the right to decide what jobs they consider to be better than no job at all. It is their sole right to decide what job is a 'decent' job. No one has the right to take away that decision-making power from desperate people. Bargaining councils are anti-constitutional and anti-democratic. It is inhuman to tell willing and relatively able people that they have nothing to offer an economy. Those who have come out against bargaining councils and the damage they do to the economy include Gill Marcus, the former governor of the South African Reserve Bank; Simon Susman, chairman of Woolworths; the Bank of America Merrill Lynch; and the International Monetary Fund.[6]

With no prospect of leaving the country, with no real education to give me the independence I thought I was going to gain through it, and with no work experience, in the 1980s I faced poverty and unemployment. Despite the legislative framework that barred black people from venturing into business, I decided that the only way I could be free under apartheid conditions was to go into business, which I did. Using business as a vehicle turned out to be the best route to freedom, the best way to escape the constraints of the apartheid laws that weighed so heavily on all of us.

Before venturing into business, I had worked for a guaranteed salary for 30 months of my life: seven months for Spar in Pretoria and 23 months for Motani Industries. In retrospect, looking at my working career in the early 1980s, with no university studies behind me and no work experience, I believe I was fortunate to have had no government deciding whether I could work and what I could be paid. My first job with Spar paid me only R175 a month as a dispatch clerk. Was I happy with the salary I was offered? Absolutely not. But that job did at least offer me the opportunity to decide for myself how to shape my future, and I committed myself fully to the opportunity. In the process I gained invaluable experience that allowed me, seven months later, to get a job at Motani paying me R100 more.

The 23 months that I worked for Motani gave me enough time to plan and shape my future strategically. I started to save money to buy a car, which I needed in order to operate as a commission salesman. Two months after buying the car, I resigned from Motani and started my entrepreneurial journey despite the apartheid legislation that sought to prevent me from working in certain areas—influx control and the Group Areas Act.

Now, more than 30 years later, I find myself again fighting for freedom, this time not for myself but for the millions of unemployed people and small businesses in our country. In a democratic South Africa I am in a situation where I have to object to laws that I find unjust. I am relieved not to have to undergo military training to challenge these unjust laws, since South Africa has a sound legal system and courts that are guided in their decisions by the rule of law. I am convinced that our legal system will not allow injustice towards our country's poorest people to continue. Credit goes to all who made it possible for us to live under this democratic dispensation, including members of our current government who led the fight against the apartheid regime. But today we can use our constitutional and human rights to correct the current wrongs in our country, and we must.

As a declared capitalist and chairman of the FMF, I decided to fight for the rights of our poor and unemployed people. The FMF has a history of claiming justice for all, especially the rights of the poorest and most vulnerable people in the country. We could not live with ourselves if we did nothing to assist the eight million poor unemployed who are being prevented from getting jobs because of our stringent and draconian labour laws.

Households and SMEs, black businesses in particular, are severely punished when they don't observe the labour laws. There is no common sense in the application of the labour laws. For these business owners and employers to understand the complicated laws, they have to study the details or pay labour experts to keep them on the right side of the law. In the 2010 Newcastle situation of factory closures because of minimum-wage disputes, it was evident that even though the workers were prepared to work at those wages and under those working conditions, their employers were punished for not adhering to the law; businesses were closed down and the workers lost their jobs. In such circumstances it is unsurprising that people choose to mechanise instead of creating employment. Mechanisation avoids adherence to restrictive labour laws.

SMEs are often 'perceived as local or regional entities that are largely technophobic, and have at best only a supporting role in international trade'.[7] Indeed, 'even in this age of globalization, SMEs . . . are still viewed as largely only effective in their domestic and, occasionally, regional markets,' says Ghanaian tech innovator Bright Simons in the *Harvard Business Review*.[8] However, according to *Oxford Economics*, SMEs operate under the same circumstances as large multinational enterprises— they too have to face 'increasing globalization, heavy competition, newly empowered customers in new markets, and fast-changing technologies ... [and] increased competition at home from rivals based outside their domestic markets'.[9] These SMEs are resisting the established stereotypes of SMEs, and internationally they are 'making major changes to their business models, products, and go-to-market strategies, and using technology to level the playing field with bigger companies. Many SMEs believe they are not only equipped to compete with larger firms, but actually have some advantages over them.'[10]

In Europe, '99% of all businesses are SMEs. Of these, 90% employ less than 10 people. Not surprisingly, two-thirds of all jobs created in the EU are created in SMEs.'[11] In the United States, 'SMEs account for 97% of the total number of exporting firms'.[12] Unfortunately, in the past two decades in South Africa, we have not seen growth of small and medium-sized black-owned businesses that comes anywhere close to the rate of growth of such businesses in other countries. 'In South Africa, SMEs contribute 56% of private sector employment and 36% of the gross domestic product.'[13] South Africa fails dismally in business and job creation, and our restrictive labour laws play a significant role in that failure, with entrepreneurship, job creation, and economic growth all being the casualties of the current labour legislation.

Bargaining councils (via union membership) supposedly employ 50% of current workers in an industry, and worker representatives negotiate wages, benefits, and other employment conditions for that particular industry. These conditions are then extended to other firms in the industry that are not party to the negotiations. Most often the negotiating parties are larger companies, and we can assume that the agreed-upon wages reflect the higher wages paid by these companies, which have incentives to increase rivals' costs, increase their own profits, and drive rivals out of the industry. The current legislation makes the Minister of Labour collusive in this discrimination.

As past chairman of the FMF, I know that our board and members were particularly frustrated by this labour legislation and the havoc it has wrought in the lives of the poor and the unemployed. It has resulted in fewer smaller firms, fewer opportunities and fewer jobs. Unemployed people lose status, skills, self-belief, and employability. Young people in particular lose on-the-job training, give up hope, and become mired in poverty. South Africa cannot allow such soul-destroying circumstances to continue. Unemployment is a cancer that eats at the vital organs of our democracy. This simply has to change.

The high level of job security and income now provided by the labour laws has had unintended consequences of preventing the unemployed from developing skills and securing jobs. This has resulted because labour laws that are suitable in large firms can have catastrophic consequences in rural areas, for small firms, and for unskilled workers. One size does not fit all. It never has. For example, in bargaining councils, once participants have agreed on terms and conditions of employment, including wage and skills, the Minister of Labour has no choice but to extend the agreements and make them enforceable for everyone else in the same industry. This makes no allowances regarding a business's geographic location in the country or for anyone's personal circumstances. Even though business owners have not participated in the negotiations or agreed to the terms and conditions of the bargaining councils, they must comply. In other words, the big guys make the rules for the little guys with absolutely no consultation or participation. That is hardly democratic.

Consequently, bargaining councils representing elites have their agreements extended to small firms and unskilled workers. In so doing, they know that many of the small firms will not be able to sustain the wages or provide the benefits stipulated in the agreements—that they cannot be competitive, that they cannot operate economically, and that disadvantaged workers will be the losers. But the councils go ahead and enforce the agreements anyway. Those who are responsible show a careless disregard for human suffering.

In 2013, after giving serious consideration to the labour legislation, the FMF decided to use the courts to compel lawmakers to review some aspects of these devastating laws. The decision was not taken lightly, but it is necessary for the future of South Africa, and the decision was taken to demonstrate our commitment and loyalty to our country. The FMF's intention is not to challenge the rights of bargaining councils, or the rights of the labour unions to represent their workers to the best of their abilities; nor are we being unpatriotic in taking the government to the highest court to stop the extension of the bargaining councils' agreements to everyone else in the industry across the country.

The FMF challenge against section 32(2) of the Labour Relations Act 66 of 1995 simply proposes that, if you did not have a say in the negotiations or agree to the terms, then you should not be bound by them. We feel as strongly as anyone about the right of collective bargaining, but where we differ from the bargaining parties is that, while we defend their rights, we also defend the rights of their competitors, especially poor and destitute fellow South Africans. The South African Reserve Bank sums matters up like this: 'Where large firms and unions agree to high standards, legal extension reduces competition and inhibits creation of new firms and their survival.'[14]

Woolworths chairman Simon Susman has noted: 'Like most businesses, we watch with deep concern the flow of restrictive, populist legislation being imposed on commerce in South Africa.'[15] The FMF simply cannot stand by and watch more people denied work because of this legislation. We believe that, by stopping this practice, we will increase the demand for labour in South Africa and bring about a dramatic decline in unemployment. All we ask is that parties to agreements should not be allowed to prescribe to the minister and that the minister should be free to extend bargaining council agreements, but must first consider the implications for non-parties. We cannot fathom how any reasonable person could disagree with this proposal. Essentially, it is a matter of choice and, more important, of who makes that choice.

If discrimination is unfair, then people should have the freedom to reject it. When people are unfairly exploited and government makes choices for them, then people's hard-won freedoms are being denied. Everyone should have the right to decide for himself or herself. This discrimination is exactly what South Africans are experiencing now. It is patronising and demeaning. The FMF court challenge re the bargaining council agreements is directed solely against the compulsory extension of the agreements to non-participating third parties, many of whom are small manufacturers and many of whom are located in rural areas with significantly high unemployment—exactly where the need for employment is the greatest. This is where the damage is done. This is what the challenge seeks to amend. It seeks the restoration of rights of small businesses and workers to make their own decisions, and to make their own choices regarding how they'll put their talents and their labour to work. It will restore the self-worth and dignity of millions who are denied employment by a well-meaning but nonetheless toxic practice. The IMF says: 'It is important to stop extending negotiated wages to other firms that were not part of the bargaining process.'[16]

It has been two years since the launch of our court challenge in the Gauteng North High Court, and, to our disappointment, our legal team is being frustrated by steps to delay this matter from being heard. I have made several public declarations that I look forward to the day when I will get to meet the Minister of Labour in an open court, where she will present her reasons for challenging the FMF action in support of small businesses and the eight million unemployed South Africans. It is clear to me that we do not have a Department of Labour that looks after the interests of the entire potential workforce. We have the arm of the labour union masquerading as a labour department. One of its tasks is to apply regulations that will keep the unemployed from competing for jobs of union members.

CHAPTER 9

UNIONS IN A FREE ECONOMY

It is somewhat perplexing that Pierre de Vos, chair of Constitutional Governance at the University of Cape Town, would term the FMF challenge a 'Quixotic venture', because the FMF is not tilting at windmills; our challenge is not idealistic.[1] The FMF labour challenge to the principle of extending bargaining council agreements to non-parties is not the first legal challenge against this legislation. However, both of the other challenges—one in the engineering industry and the other in the clothing industry—relate solely to those particular industries. The FMF labour challenge seeks to include 'all industries governed by bargaining councils where there is extension to non-parties', and it is the first challenge that is based entirely on constitutional grounds.[2] The FMF labour challenge proposes that the government cannot assign statutory regulatory powers to private individuals, since it violates the Constitution, and that, due to a distortion of the provisions of majority rule, the minority is empowered to compel the majority to comply with terms and conditions of employment.

The bargaining council agreement legislation that is currently in place in South Africa was once practised in New Zealand, Australia, the United States and Germany. The US Supreme Court outlawed the practice. The International Labour Organization's 2011 study on collective bargaining concluded that 'what emerges is that in an environment of high inequality as in SA, collective bargaining has become a key mechanism for redistribution; thus it has been more effective in protecting earnings than in saving jobs'.[3]

However, not everyone saw the challenge in the light of progress and freedom, and surprisingly fierce criticism came mainly from the labour unions, whose criticism was direct and threatening. Failing to see that the FMF labour challenge, if successful, would boost jobs and membership of their unions, they went so far as to call it a direct attack against their workers' rights, which is ludicrous. In their press statement, the COSATU-affiliated Southern African Clothing and Textile Workers Union (SACTWU) claimed that the FMF's labour challenge was 'a direct attack on core worker rights [which are] fundamental human rights', and regarded the challenge as a 'brutal attack against our country's democratically legislated industrial relations system, in particular its collective bargaining architecture'.[4] Of course, in true union style, they called for resistance, stating '[such] resistance should not be confined to the legal corridors, but also fought on the streets. We will mobilise to resist the reactionary, right wing economic and destructive intentions of the Free Market Foundation.'[5] Additionally,

SACTWU sent a directive to members in their sectors to disassociate themselves from the FMF, and, as part of their Conditions of Employment for 2014–2016, to sign an agreement that they would not allow the FMF to take the matter to court. Such a prescription and incitement to violence is not the sign of a healthy democracy.

These tactics are nothing short of intimidation. And far from improving the worker environment for South Africans, they seek to destroy it, by denying hundreds of thousands of citizens participation in the economy, an economy in which they are currently prevented from participating because of this single draconian labour law. What is tragic is that the unions perceive free-market liberalists to be against the rights of workers. This could not be more erroneous. As FMF founder Leon Louw says: 'No ideology espouses the rights of workers, including the right to form unions, more unambiguously than free-market liberalism.'[6]

More than anything, this labour challenge seeks to ensure the freedom and prosperity that only free economies offer—'freedom of association, freedom of contract, civil liberty and the rule of law'.[7] The FMF is not against organised labour and labour unions; all citizens have the right to belong to whatever organisation they choose to represent them. What is important is that workers have the freedom to negotiate, that they act lawfully, and that they honour their employment contracts.

Free marketers acknowledge the important role of unions, not only in labour negotiations but also in other contexts, such as representing members in service delivery and providing pension, medical, and investment schemes. What liberal free marketers seek is to prevent labour laws that drive and support the agendas of unions against other non-unionised and vulnerable parties. The Marikana massacre of 2012 was fuelled by the tripartite antagonism among striking workers, the National Union of Mineworkers (NUM), and Lonmin management.

The Marikana or Lonmin strike took place between 11 and 16 August 2012, marking the 25-year anniversary of a nationwide South African miners' strike.[8] Inquiries into the strike and the subsequent massacre have resulted in confusion regarding who fired the first shots, but on 16 August 44 people died, mainly striking mineworkers, and approximately 78 additional workers were injured. According to the *Daily Maverick* investigation, the violence started on 8 August 2012 and was attributable directly to NUM. 'On Wednesday 8 August, some rock drill operators (RDOs) from various Lonmin mines had a mass meeting demanding a significant salary increase. The NUM leaders who were present categorically refused to support the strike, despite the union's stated mission to promote and represent the interests of its members.'[9] On 9 August 2012 thousands of RDOs from the Lonmin mines 'came together as workers, not as a union', and congregated at the Lonmin-owned football stadium, where they decided to approached Lonmin directly, since NUM had refused to represent them.[10] On 10 August the workers marched on Lonmin offices, but management refused to engage with the workers and told them to return to NUM for representation.

With both the mine and NUM refusing to meet the workers, approximately 3 000 RDOs and miners decided to strike.

On 11 August the miners went to the NUM offices in Wonderkop, offices that are shared with the SACP and ANC, to present their memorandum calling for a R12 500 minimum wage for all miners. Members present during this march were mostly NUM members, but there were also a few members of the Association of Mineworkers and Construction Union (AMCU). Was this protest an instance of NUM members rebelling against their own leadership, or a case of inter-union rivalry? Perhaps the Farlam Commission will be able to shed more light on this. However, the *Mail & Guardian* reported that once the strikers 'were about 100–150 metres away from the NUM office, eyewitnesses, both participants in the march and informal traders in and around a nearby taxi rank, reported without exception that "top five" NUM leaders and other shop stewards, between 15 and 20 in all, came out of the office and began shooting at the protesting strikers somewhere in the vicinity of the Wonderkop taxi rank,' and claimed that 'NUM personnel shot at the protesters without warning or provocation. The miners were clearly ambushed by their union representatives.'[11] Two deaths were reported that day.

While the Marikana massacre that ensued when police killed dozens of mineworkers is reprehensible and has been the major focus of attention, the abovementioned scenario at the start of the strike also requires reflection and comment. Why did NUM refuse to represent the workers? Whose agenda directed their refusal? And what reason fuelled them to attack their own members? These are surely questions that union workers and the Farlam Commission should be asking. As Jeremy Gordin, director of the University of the Witwatersrand's Justice Project, has observed: 'I think that in a certain way the carnage at Marikana mine is about union warfare—and I think it is very significant … I don't think a rock-drill operator in an industry under pressure is much interested in their [union and ANC] politicking. So he and his buddies decide to get their own union going. NUM doesn't like that; nor does COSATU; nor does the ANC. I believe the claims by AMCU "officials" that Lonmin management has a cozy relationship with NUM; it's the way things have been done for quite a while now.'[12] Clearly Marikana is a damning example of a union not acting in the best interests of its members. Indeed, if union officials were concerned with their membership's employment conditions, they too would support the labour law challenge instead of vilifying it.

Fortunately, common sense prevails among those creators of employment, and we are encouraged by the groundswell of support. Gerhard Papenfus from the National Employers' Association of South Africa has supported the FMF's labour challenge and refers to the current section 32 of the Labour Relations Act as 'akin to a weapon for Big Business against its small competitors'. He is hugely supportive of the Free Market Foundation's attack on it through the courts. Papenfus believes this could be the crack which breaks the dyke of South Africa's destructive labour legislation.'[13]

It is only when labour unions and government really grasp the consequences of the current legislation that business will flourish. As the FMF has suggested, failure to address the labour laws will result in mechanisation, so it's no surprise that even big business is seeking to mechanise. Three years of experiencing strike action has taken its toll on the mining industry, and there is a push by management of the top mining houses to resolve labour issues by mechanising. 'Labour militancy is dictating our push to mechanisation and boardrooms will rubber stamp this stuff,' said Peter Major, a fund manager at Cadiz Corporate Solutions.[14]

Anglo American Platinum's Bathopele mine has retrenched rock drillers, and hydraulic machines have replaced them. The world's top three producers, Implats, Amplats, and Lonmin, which experienced a five-month wage strike by AMCU workers, have shown 'an unprecedented example of cooperation in an industry that has long been fiercely competitive and secretive' by joining Joy Global 'to develop rock-cutting technology, which would remove the need for blasting and rock drilling'.[15]

The reason behind the mechanisation drive is attributable to the ongoing strife and violence between NUM and AMCU and to government's quest to increase safety and 'move away from the labour-intensive, low-wage model rooted in the apartheid era'.[16] Could this response by South Africa's major industry have a trickle-down effect on other business sectors? If it does, South Africa faces critical job shortages. It is a stark reality that South Africa's labour relations environment is in crisis. We cannot continue on this path. South Africa cannot afford these damaging and increasingly violent strikes. Negotiation and dialogue are degenerating into dangerously entrenched positions from which there can be no winners, only many losers, most importantly the unemployed.

The labour challenge was launched in the North Gauteng High Court on 5 March 2013 against the Minister of Labour, the Minister of Constitutional Development, and all 46 bargaining councils. Immediately after this launch, the Minister of Constitutional Development responded that the department was happy to comply with any court ruling, but to our surprise, the Minister of Labour, whom this challenge is about to empower, responded by claiming to oppose the challenge.

Since the launch of this important challenge, the FMF has been faced with a series of delaying tactics to avoid the case being heard in an open court of law. The strategy being used is to invite various COSATU affiliates to challenge the case individually, asking the courts to allow them to be included as defendants. All the respondents, including the Minister of Labour, keep referring to the FMF's labour challenge as an attack on the rights of the 8.3 million unemployed South Africans and small business owners. This delay only reinforces the FMF's resolve to push for the day when they will meet the Minister of Labour in an open court of law, to explain to our unemployed fellow South Africans why the Minister of Labour is not prepared to consider their plight. The FMF has full confidence in our judiciary to grant a hearing and is ready to accept the legal outcome.

What is most disturbing about these delaying tactics is our government's participation in openly disregarding the application of the rule of law. How abnormal is it that a civil society organisation is challenging an important aspect of the Constitution, and during the process the government is the party frustrating the application of the rule of law? We live in a country that is currently experiencing the lowest rate of growth in Africa, with one of the highest unemployment rates in the developing world, and we have a government that frustrates efforts to stir the economy for positive growth. This clearly demonstrates where our government's focus is directed; it is solely interested in protecting the agendas of COSATU and its leadership, not the interests of union members.

South Africans fought and defeated the evil system of apartheid so that we could all enjoy real freedom. This forced domination by labour surely acts against the spirit and intent of our Constitution. I have made a commitment to my children that I am not prepared to passively watch what happens, but do nothing about it. My fellow South Africans, in particular the vulnerable, unskilled, uneducated, and unemployed, also deserve to be respected. We who have benefitted from the end of apartheid need to use our privileged position in society to demonstrate to the marginalised that we care. I grew up believing that white South Africans were evil because a majority of them never cared about our plight; they did not use their privileged position to make a difference to the lives of their fellow citizens. Today I am driven by that fear and knowledge. The

idea of another Herman growing up in a desperate environment, now believing that the problem is attributable to all of
us privileged people, black and white, is something I want to
avoid. Capitalists like myself need to demonstrate proactively
to all fellow human beings that we do care, that we are committed to a just and fair society.

CHAPTER 10

AN OPEN OPPORTUNITY SOCIETY

Since 1999 I have felt less than satisfied, on many levels, that the ANC is the party worthy of my continued support. I became disenchanted with the leadership and how that leadership was attained; and the party's policies and practices seemed less inclined towards the country's citizens and a strong economy and more inclined towards supporting the upper echelons of the party's membership and a socialist agenda. I reached the stage where I no longer believed I was voting for the same party that was founded on the principles enshrined in the liberal South African Constitution and the party that had liberated the country and given all South Africans a sense of common nationality.

I realised that I had to join a party that could achieve the power necessary to bring about vital changes if our country was to avoid going the way of other failing and underperforming African countries. In my opinion, the Democratic Alliance is the only political party capable of delivering a better life for all

South Africans. Like all political parties, it is not perfect. It faces internal and external challenges. But unlike the ANC, which is dismissive of critique or dismisses it outright, the DA leaders are aware of their shortcomings and are eager to engage in dialogue to foster changes. I don't expect perfection in a political party, because human beings by nature are not perfect. I look for a party that is most closely aligned to my value system and beliefs.

The DA's objective is an 'Open Opportunity Society for All' and its economic and social policies are engineered to increase growth and job creation. The party's vision is that South Africa becomes a 'society in which every person is free, secure and equal, where everyone has the opportunity to improve the quality of their life and pursue their dreams'.[1] These are principles that I believe are closely allied to our Constitution.

The DA is essentially an amalgamation of different parties and movements that have joined forces over the years with the aim of achieving an open opportunity society for all South Africans. When the ANC and other liberation organisations were unbanned, negotiations for real political change in South Africa were initiated and the Democratic Party (DP) played a pivotal role in negotiating an interim Constitution that was closely allied to the principles promulgated by the Progressive Party in 1959. In the first post-apartheid election in 1994, the DP won 1.7% of the vote at national level, and over the next five years under Tony Leon's leadership, the DP fought to legitimise itself as the official opposition to the ANC. In the 1995 municipal elections the DP started to show growth, and by the 1999 general election, the DP's share of the national vote had increased to 9%, taking over from the National Party to become the largest opposition to the ANC. In 2000 the DP merged with the Federal Alliance and the New National Party to form the Democratic Alliance. However, in 2001, the New National Party leader Marthinus van Schalkwyk led his party into an alliance with the ANC. In the 2004 general election the DA gained 12.3% of the vote, and its support grew in eight of the nine provinces. This result confirmed the DA's status as the only feasible opposition to the ANC. In the 2006 local government elections, the DA increased its national share of the vote by a further 4% to 16.3%. It gained more representatives in all six of the metropolitan councils, the most important of which was the Cape Town Metro, where the DA increased its share of the vote to 41.9% (ANC: 38%), and the DA member of Parliament and national spokesperson Helen Zille was elected mayor. Her two-vote majority enabled the DA to form a governing coalition of seven parties. In the 2011 local government election, the DA won 57% of the vote in the Western Cape, and the DA currently controls 28 municipalities across the country. In the 2014 general election the DA won 22.23% of the national vote.[2] These figures attest to the significant support that the DA continues to garner, year after year, election after election.

The figures are not just meaningless numbers. The people living in the areas where the DA has triumphed have seen positive changes in their quality of life and measurable improvements in service delivery, specifically in the Western Cape. Recently the DA was criticised for the shocking state of the Cape Town railway station. Attacks like these are intended to undermine the DA's administration in the province. However, most people are not even sure under whose jurisdiction the railway station falls; in this case it is under the jurisdiction of the national government, and one can hardly expect the ANC to fund maintenance and upgrades in a province they do not dominate. They would much rather fund projects in the provinces or municipalities where they want to retain power.

The DA's principles are constitutionally based, and I agree with every one of them. However, I would like to highlight those that appeal particularly, because we are not seeing these same principles being upheld by the ANC. The key principles are:

- ❏ 'The supremacy of the South African Constitution and the rule of law.
- ❏ A judiciary that is independent.
- ❏ Representative and accountable government elected on the basis of universal adult suffrage.
- ❏ The clear division between the ruling party and the state.
- ❏ Respect for the right of a vibrant civil society and a free media to function independently.
- ❏ The rejection of violence and intimidation as a political instrument.
- ❏ The right of all people to private ownership and to participate freely in the market economy.

☐ The progressive realisation of access to housing, health services and social security for all people who are unable to help themselves.'[3]

In previous chapters I have tackled the ANC on their failed policies. I believe it is prudent to examine the DA policies that are aligned to my vision for South Africa. The DA states that in the years since our democratic transition, 'the ANC has not been willing or able to fundamentally change this basic structure. South Africa remains a country of insiders and outsiders with Big Government, Big Unions and some anti-competitive Big Businesses on one side, and millions of ordinary ... South Africans on the other.'[4]

The DA's economic policy is stated in its Plan for Growth and Jobs (2014), which contains plans to reform the South African economy, a reformation that cannot transpire unless the vast numbers of unemployed become employed. This simply has to be South Africa's primary priority, both morally and economically. Economic inclusion has not been realised, as we have seen in the unemployment figures I have given and the resulting social consequences (see Chapter 5). The DA includes the following elements as characteristics required to enable growth: provide leadership, accountability in managing public funds, incentivise businesses to create jobs, ensure that labour laws support job creation, enable the creation and growth of SMEs, broaden participation in the economy, invest in economic infrastructure, invest in knowledge, increase investment and savings, and boost trade.

The DA's practical recommendations to boost the economy are detailed in their 2014 election manifesto. It promotes working with the private sector to provide affordable, quality health care and to create a million internships to provide work experience for young job seekers. It is estimated that R30 billion could be saved by rooting out and firing corrupt officials, and that an investment of R10 billion could accelerate land reform and provide support and training for emerging farmers. Students who cannot afford to be educated could access education if the National Student Financial Aid Scheme budget were increased to R16 billion. SMEs would be created if limiting legislation was scrapped, and support and training were provided for these companies. Public works could provide seven million opportunities for the unemployed. To increase competition and decrease costs, inefficient state monopolies need to be dismantled and their shares distributed to ordinary citizens. If 10% of the GDP were invested in communication infrastructure, it would develop sufficiently to meet the demands of the economy.

The following key policy decisions that the 2015 DA congress made are significant to economic development in South Africa. First, it advocated that state land held in trust by former Bantustan tribal chiefs be released to those people who live and work on it and that they be given the title deeds to confirm their ownership. Second, it advocated broad-based ownership of the property that black people occupy in urban townships (including informal settlements) to allow previously disadvantaged people to participate in the economy. Third, a change to the electoral system was proposed, whereby instead of all members of Parliament being elected from party lists, 75% of the country's MPs would be directly elected by their constituencies, and the other 25% would be a result of proportional representation.

These economic policies attest to a party that realises its responsibility to practical and implementable solutions. They are formulated with the people at the heart of their consideration.

The party's labour policy is of significant relevance to me, as it confirms my belief that without a marriage between labour reform and educational reform, our economic future is doomed.

Governance is a bugbear issue for critics of the ANC, as we find ourselves in a situation where governance is laughable. The DA realises that governance, as with all policy proposals, must focus on improving the lives of South Africans. Allied to the changes required in the areas of unemployment, inequality, and poverty, the government and all state organs must deliver on their responsibility to the country. If we are to achieve the effective, transparent, and accountable government that the Constitution promises, then we must have a government that responds to the needs of its people instead of its party members, that delivers efficient services, and that is committed to spending public money for the public. 'The State of Management Practices in the Public Service 2012 report released by the Performance Monitoring and Evaluation Department confirmed that the DA-led Western Cape Government has the best public service management practices in the country.'[5]

The DA proposes the following to ensure a more efficient government: to limit political interference in public administration, to strengthen accountability, to ensure that best-practice models are emulated, to ensure interdepartmental co-operation, to streamline government administration to avoid unnecessary bureaucracies, to clarify the roles of traditional leaders, and to ensure that effective policies currently in force are more effective.

Crime is the most talked-about social problem. It is almost impossible to function effectively when one has to live in a constant state of fear, and this is not an imagined fear. With 47 murders occurring every day during the 2013–2014 period, it is very real.[6] Crime strips South Africa of talented people. It creates suspicion between people and breaks down national harmony. According to the StatsSA Victims of Crime Survey 2013/14, respondents in a third of households avoid being unaccompanied in open spaces for fear of crime, those in a quarter of households don't allow their children to play freely or unsupervised, and only 14% of respondents feel safe to go out in their area after dark.[7] In the same survey, 64.1% considered social and economic development to be the most effective way to reduce crime, 20% felt that resources should be allocated to law enforcement, and 15.6% believed that resources directed to the judiciary or courts would effectively reduce crime. The DA's proposed policy is aligned to the public's perceptions of crimes, seeking to have a well-trained, properly equipped, responsive police service that would be able to respond to personal threats against South

African citizens. The DA believes an independent judiciary that is well resourced and managed would ensure that criminals were given a fair and speedy trial and were appropriately punished if found guilty. It is necessary to implement a correctional service system that offers criminals effective rehabilitation to ensure that criminality is reduced over time. Finally, the DA proposes a support system that is cognisant of victims' needs, ensuring that the response to the criminality in South Africa is a multifaceted, intentional, and focused response. We need to live in a society where citizens understand the implications of their criminal activities, and communities feel confident that guilty criminals will be punished. The DA has acknowledged that unless social and economic upliftment takes place, South Africans who are uneducated and unemployed feel limited in their ability to be productive members of society and turn to crime instead. Every South African has the ability to detect and report crime, and no matter which government is in power, it is our civic duty to be alert and safe in reporting crime.

Crime may top the agenda in much civic conversation, but land is another issue that provokes strong feeling. Whenever the EFF or landgrabbers start whinging about land they are owed, South Africans get really hot under the collar. And why not? Who among us wants to think about land we have worked to buy being taken away from us? Regardless of whether it is land you've inherited or land you've bought in the last five years, all you're interested in is the risk of being dispossessed. With land issues being such a contested issue because of our historical

dispossession, land reform has to be a carefully considered programme. The DA recognises that racial dispossession has created 'patterns of ownership that exclude the majority of South
Africans from land assets and inclusion in rural economies'.[8]
They understand that land and its usage are tied to food production and security, and that land reform policies must take
into consideration an affordable and continued supply of food,
if we are to strike the balance that the economy requires. But
ultimately the DA supports a land reform process that is intent on economic inclusion of the rural populations, that will
support growth in the agricultural sector, and that will achieve
reparation and compensation in rural communities. The ANC
has tried to establish black commercial farms without success;
it has not supported an agricultural sector that can maintain
food security, and it has failed to assure the rights of 'millions
of South Africans living on state-owned communal land, or in
addressing the urgent land pressures in urban areas' in any significant way. To achieve what the ANC has failed to achieve,
the DA proposes: 'We must shift the focus of land reform from
meeting targets to meeting needs.'[9]

The announcement of my decision to join the DA was met
with both approval and criticism, for which I am delighted. I
want my involvement to create discussion. I hope it will encourage like-minded South Africans to take an active interest
in the future of our country, since that is what a democracy is
for. My decision was influenced not only by discussions with
other dissatisfied South Africans; rather it was influenced by

my deep distress at the status quo of the country. When I joined the DA as an ordinary card-carrying member, I did not aspire to an elected position in the party; instead I was forthright in stating my intention to promote the DA's policies in all my interactions with all South Africans. I want to demonstrate to the voting public that the party is not just a white party but a party for all South Africans, and a party of the future.

Ultimately my membership of the DA is an endorsement of the principles of non-racialism, a healthy capitalist market economy that delivers jobs, a smaller and more effective government dedicated to a constructive partnership with business, and eventually a direct democracy where all politicians are held personally accountable for their performance and behaviour. I support a free-enterprise economy because capitalism is the true creator of jobs and the best way of spreading prosperity, particularly among the less privileged.

Many black voters veer away from the DA because of being under the misapprehension that the DA is a white party intent on protecting white interests, while others have rejected the DA out of fear, based on insinuations by political opponents who falsely suggest that a vote for the DA is a vote to reinstate the apartheid laws and a vote for white supremacy. It is mystifying that some parties have to resort to fear mongering to ensure that they get a vote, but that reflects the mendacious nature of some politicians. The race issue is precisely one of the reasons I joined the DA. Why do people consider a vote for the DA as a black vs white issue? If a vote for the ANC is considered a

vote for blacks, then we need to do some serious voter education. When critics refer to me as a coconut, a *kleva* black, or a
wannabe white, I'm really not affected at all; in fact I see these
references as nothing more than diversionary tactics. The fact
that they focus on denigrating me and playing the race card,
rather than on the appalling issues that need to be addressed,
tells me that these people need to be informed about what the
party really stands for.

The party in power should adhere to the tenets of the
Constitution, which guarantees equality for all—not benefits
for some at the expense of others. In reality the DA, not the
ANC, has become the party of Mandela's dream of a rainbow
nation.

The ANC's Twenty Year Review insists that gains have been
made since 1994, and while there are certain gains, I strongly
contest that they have a good story to tell. As I discussed in
every chapter so far, the ANC's service delivery is disputable. I
only have to look at service delivery in my own hometown to see
that all is not what the ANC would have us believe. GaRamotse
received water, electricity, and tarred roads subsequent to the
1994 election, but a drive through the village today paints a disturbing reality. The water supply is sporadic at best; the roads
are in a chronic state of disrepair. The feeding schemes are a
welcome alleviation for hungry bellies but are not uplifting
in the long term, and the state of education is diabolical. How
can 16 million people on social grants be considered a success?
Social grants are not successes; they're social failures and an

utter disgrace. Social grants make absolutely no contribution to upliftment; all they do is keep people trapped in the quagmire of desperate poverty. It infuriates me. While the masses starve, our government is gorging itself on public funds, bloating its numbers, and using the money for service delivery to buy political support and patronage.

It's sickening, but it's not unstoppable. Poor South Africans simply have to realise that our votes are keeping us poor. When we finally accept that the ANC is spending the money on themselves instead of on the poor, we may stand a chance of making the changes from which we will all benefit. Poor communities need voter education so as to make informed decisions regarding their future. As chairman of the FMF, I clashed regularly with COSATU over labour issues. They criticised my pro-business capitalist stance, accusing me of a class war on workers, which couldn't be further from the truth. The labour unions, however, are more attuned to attending to the leadership's interest than to creating jobs for members. By the same token, the ANC is intent on creating wealth for its leadership.

Since I joined the DA, there has been speculation as to my intentions. Was I manoeuvring to contest leadership in the party? Absolutely not. I supported and endorsed Mmusi Maimane's bid for leadership. Instead, my intention is to promote the party and its ideals in my sphere of influence, to champion it in my daily dealings with South Africans from all echelons. I want to eliminate the misconception of the DA as a white party; it simply is not true. Its members are by no means all whites, and its policies are constitutionally based, resulting in its gains benefitting all South Africans.

It is not only the black population who need to become more politically involved. I would like to see South Africa's white population becoming more publicly involved in the nation's issues as well. Whoever does not like something should use the Constitution to protest against it or speak up against injustice collectively and demand reform. Social media rants will not achieve the changes the electorate would like to see; the only thing that will result in change is action. Ignore the racist or elitist labels that will be attached to you for taking a stand, in the same way I have to ignore the slurs attached to me. Focus on the issues instead, so that progress and change can come about.

It is for the reasons described here that I avail myself of every opportunity to punt capitalism for reform and promote the DA as the party of change for South Africa. I urge fellow South Africans to do the same. Add your voice of discontent to ensure a South Africa that delivers for all of its people.

CHAPTER 11

GETTING EDUCATION RIGHT

In 1953 the dastardly Prime Minister Verwoerd said: 'The Bantu must be guided to serve his own community in all respects. There is no place for him in the European community above the level of certain forms of labour.'[1] This was the political environment into which I was born and under which I grew up, fully conscious of what Verwoerd meant for me and my race. I knew my success was dependent on proving the National Party and its racist policies wrong. Notwithstanding these major challenges, I grew up wanting the best education for myself. Our knowledge of the Nats' plan to withhold appropriate education ended up being the tool some of us used to motivate ourselves to work to achieve.

Regrettably, our education in the main has not changed. The tragedy is that most people are not even conscious of the poor quality of education being offered by our public education system. Black children still participate in an unequal education system that does not equip them for economic inclusion. The dire state of South African education means that poor black children will have less access to the economy, and this should set alarm bells ringing. If the South African government does not make education and skills training its number-one priority, then how are we going to address the triple challenge of poverty, unemployment, and inequality? And how are we going to strengthen the economy? Our education system is the fragile root of our economy, and we simply have to recognise that the failure to make meaningful changes to our education system will result in a failed country.

Yes, we inherited a dysfunctional education system born of apartheid's race-based division of resources. Yes, the ANC has faced huge challenges in providing educational facilities and levelling the access to the most basic educational amenities. But now we must examine the current state of education, more than 20 years after democracy arrived.

It is encouraging that the government's 2014 Medium Term Expenditure Framework lists quality basic education as its number-one priority.[2] However, it doesn't go nearly far enough to address the fact that businesses need skilled people. A basic education does not suffice, and 'a skilled and capable workforce to support an inclusive growth path' is well down the list as priority number five.[3] While this gives us an idea of the government's social priorities, let's establish exactly how much is invested in education in South Africa in relation to other sectors; this is an important investigation, since it shows where the government's financial priorities lie.

INVESTMENT IN EDUCATION COMPARED WITH OTHER SECTORS

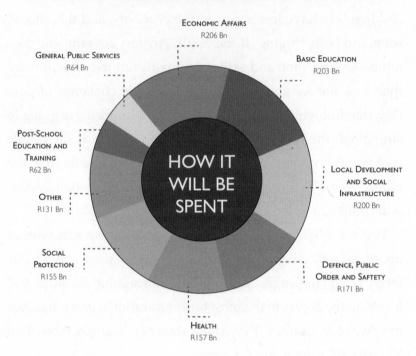

ECONOMIC AFFAIRS
R206 Bn

GENERAL PUBLIC SERVICES
R64 Bn

BASIC EDUCATION
R203 Bn

POST-SCHOOL
EDUCATION AND
TRAINING
R62 Bn

HOW IT
WILL BE
SPENT

LOCAL DEVELOPMENT
AND SOCIAL
INFRASTRUCTURE
R200 Bn

OTHER
R131 Bn

SOCIAL
PROTECTION
R155 Bn

DEFENCE, PUBLIC
ORDER AND SAFTETY
R171 Bn

HEALTH
R157 Bn

Source: South African Treasury[4]

In terms of education spending, 15.04% of the budget has been allocated to basic education, and only 4.4% has been allocated to post-school training and education.[5] The latter amount is not sufficient to resolve the issue of untrained and unskilled employees. The number of children enrolled in primary education increases every year, and 98% of South African children attend primary school.[6] However, the rate of graduation from high school is disappointing and alarming: it is estimated that 75% of children entering Grade 1 do not complete Grade 12.[7]

The challenge of ensuring we have committed, professional

teaching staff and adequate educational resources contin-ues to plague the sector. The major source of this problem is the dominance of trade union interference and control of our public education system. COSATU, a senior partner in the tripartite alliance, through the South African Democratic Teachers' Union, should take full responsibility for the cur-rent poor state of public schooling in South Africa. A Human Sciences Research Council study found that 20% of teachers are absent on Mondays and Fridays, and absenteeism increases to 33% at the end of the month. Teachers in black schools teach for an average of only three-and-a-half hours a day, compared with six-and-a-half hours a day in former white schools. What this means in real terms for a child in one of these black schools is 'a difference of three years' schooling in total'.[8] It is estimated that only 71% of children who should be in Grade 6 are literate, and only 58.6% of children in this same group are numerate.[9]

In an attempt to reconcile the social discrepancies in educa-tion, the government has taken to providing feeding schemes in primary schools. I have already noted that I find this a dubious inclusion in the education system; in effect the government strips parents of the dignity of providing for their children. I don't be-lieve a government can put its finger in the dyke of education to prevent the spillover into poverty. Curriculum changes have been made, and syllabi reflect the changes in content, but the cost of these changes has bitten significantly into the pie of education spending. Yet the changes are not keeping our children in school. Failure to graduate has not been improved in any significant way.

How can we expect children to remain in schools that do not equip them with the basic skills required to advance them through the system and into working life? Martin Prew of the Centre for Education Policy Development lays the blame for insufficient teacher development on the ANC. In the mid-1990s the government closed the country's teaching colleges, believing that universities could offer better professional development. Anastasia Krystallidis, the executive head at the independent SAHETI School, notes that 'the poor calibre of teachers is a deep malaise. What we have is a dumbing down of teachers. Teachers must realise that they are the key to success (in basic education). They should take far greater academic responsibility.'[10]

But are teachers responsible for poor performance, or is this attributable to leadership? Where determined principals motivate and empower staff to do their jobs well, impoverished schools achieve good results despite their lack of resources. While we cannot ignore the importance of professional staff, we have to acknowledge that there are many factors contributing to a failing education system and that none of these factors should be seen in isolation. They are all part of the matrix resulting in an education system in crisis. The contributing factors include (but are not limited to) social problems that spill over into education—children who are on drugs, unplanned teenage pregnancies, the unaffordability of educating a child, and disciplinary problems.

In an attempt to improve the secondary school graduation rate, the government has reduced the pass rate. Currently students have to achieve 40% to pass their home language and mathematics and 30% to pass other subjects in order to be awarded a National Senior Certificate. This unacceptably low pass rate directly disadvantages learners competing for positions in tertiary education institutions. University of the Free State Vice-Chancellor Professor Jonathan Jansen and other educationalists have pushed for the pass rate to be increased to 50%. David Hopwood, CEO of Save the Children South Africa, believes that 'change is possible if we work together to build a movement for quality education. We need children, parents and communities to harness their energies and work with the Government to radically improve the quality of education in our country.'[11]

We also need to consider the administration, or should I say maladministration, in the education sector. Educational resources are not being used efficiently. Textbooks are not arriving at schools, and teachers have to cope with the lack of resources. Corruption exists in the tender sector of education. Bureaucracy frustrates the time management of teachers, whose time should be spent on teaching rather than administration. Tragically, what emerges from all this is an uneducated population of youths who can never be employed because they lack skills, and although the several factors noted here all have some bearing, I regard the government's appalling legislated intervention between employer and employees as the key problem. Yielding to COSATU imperatives means teachers and schools simply are not properly accountable to public needs.

Tertiary education comprises both academic and skills training. To focus first on academic tertiary education: the historically black universities have been allowed to languish, and black students have migrated to the historically white universities. Despite the fact that student enrolment at South African tertiary institutions 'has almost doubled, increasing from 495 356 students (universities, technikons and teachers' training colleges) in 1994 to 953 373 students (public universities and universities of technology) in 2012', the universities still face criticism that they have not transformed in a way that meets the needs of a democracy in improving social equity and meeting the country's economic development needs.[12]

I understand the need for South African universities to transform to reflect their current student body, such that students can develop their own identity. However, what I don't understand is why the government did not invest in the historically black universities to create additional centres of excellence where students could forge their own idea of what their identity as students means and what the university's function for them should be. Transformation does not come about because we demand it; it comes about democratically where the protocols of discipline and negotiation are observed. If we want our education system to evolve, it must be a negotiated transformation, not simply one where we yield to the loudest voices and most aggressive stances.

Academic staff should not be employed on the basis of their paper credentials alone. Obviously they should be experts in their field, but there are additional considerations. The content they share should be reflective of the body of knowledge in a field, it should be relevant to current conversations about that content, and they should be able to impart it in a way that is interesting, meaningful, and inspirational. I understand that racial equity in university teaching staff has not yet been attained, but if a university is a centre of excellence, then the teaching staff it appoints should be committed primarily to teaching, not appointed because a crony has supported their employment, and not in an attempt to secure tenure because they want a good retirement plan, nor because the teaching position offers them research opportunities to further their academic careers, and most certainly not based on race. Teaching is a vocation, and every teacher's first obligation must be to the students.

Ultimately, says Saleem Badat in his assessment of transformation in higher education since 1994: 'Our task is to continue to cultivate what Harvey Kaye calls "prophetic memory"... : remembrance—of our unjust and traumatic past; critique—of the inequalities and injustices that continue to blight our democracy; consciousness—that our history teaches that nothing is gained without creativity, boldness and struggle; imagination—to conceive of new ways of being and acting; and desire—to shape our destiny and remake our society and our universities.'[13]

Tertiary skills education is nowhere near realising the output that commerce and industry requires. We can talk numbers and statistics, but what cannot be ignored is the fact that our tertiary skills education sector is not producing sufficiently skilled people. South Africa does not have enough government institutions to cope with demand, and many of the private institutions are not providing graduates with sufficient and efficient skills to take their place in commerce and industry. Some of the private institutions are not accredited, charge parents outrageous fees, and employ incompetent staff to provide students with less-than-adequate skills, and everybody is a loser—parents waste money they can ill afford, and, most tragically, their children emerge without the necessary skills to offer an employer. And that is part of how we end up in the dangerous jam of frustrated employers and, as earlier noted, an astronomical youth unemployment rate of more than 50%.

Poverty and education are irretrievably entwined. We will never build a strong, economically independent nation without better education, and we can never achieve an effective education sector without investing in it. The government simply has to recognise the enormous part that education plays in poverty eradication and, conversely, the role that inadequate education plays in perpetuation of the poverty cycle.

I honestly thought that by now, two decades into our new-found democracy, we would have an educated South African society capable of running this modern economy efficiently. Instead, serious intervention in education is still required, not only at the tertiary level but at the primary and secondary levels as well. Our country should have established early-learning centres in every corner of our townships and villages, preparing our children at this initial stage of their development. Such intervention will prepare them to face tertiary education with far greater ease, as is the case in successful countries. The main reason we experience high levels of university failure lies in the inadequacy of the formative experiences of these children.

While providing such an educational environment, we must also simultaneously embark on normalising our communities. Children cannot flourish and reach their potential when reared in dysfunctional environments. They need and deserve stability during their early development. The critical point here is to allow and to enable parents to work and provide for them. Our high unemployment rate is toxic, countering the normal development of society. We cannot expect parents to exercise full responsibility for their children when they are unable even to provide a decent living. South Africa needs to embark on a major programme to encourage and support small business in providing employment for this current uneducated and unskilled potential labour force. We need political leadership capable of inspiring the nation to focus on the future, leadership prepared to invest in future generations. Sustainable success is not going to be achieved overnight. In fact, sustainable successes are normally achieved only over more than a generation, and we need to prepare South Africans to adopt such an approach. A shotgun approach will yield only the kind of results we have achieved so far, leaving us poor and blaming everybody else for the government's failure.

CHAPTER 12

HOW CITIZENS BUILD A NATION

When we celebrate a 21st birthday we're celebrating independence, maturity, and the celebrant's ability to stand on his or her own two feet. In 2015 our country celebrated 21 years of democracy. If we think back to 1994, most of us remember Nelson Mandela proclaiming the birth of a new Constitution and with it his vision of a prospering rainbow nation.[1]

Unfortunately, today that rainbow has been darkened by clouds of discontent. We have to concentrate to remember how exciting it felt to be united by a new Constitution, a new flag, a new national anthem, a world statesman who made us proud, and sports teams that made us all proud to be South African. These were all signs that we had embraced democracy and were on a path of nation-building..

Nation-building seeks to unify people within the country so that it remains sustainable and politically stable. To be a legitimate democratic state, South Africa had to construct a new nation, and it was hoped that this nation-building would be realised through popular majority rule, as is right and democratic.

Post-1994 South Africa had challenging times ahead as we sought to reshape a country forged by colonial powers that had little regard for integration. We also had to revitalise a country that was exhausted and impoverished by 48 years of apartheid rule by the National Party. We needed to construct a national identity by unifying different ethnic groups into a nation, exactly the reverse of the apartheid government's divide-and-rule policy of ethnically isolated homelands for different tribes. We aimed at unifying all South Africans so that we could have a cohesive and equal society.

But we only have to pick up a newspaper, watch television, follow social media, or eavesdrop on conversations to know that South Africa has not achieved that cohesive and equal society. How could that be? The intention was there. The Constitution supported harmony and goodwill. Why has it not been achieved? How do you build a nation?

The main basic requirements of creating an integrated society are a common identity and ideology. From the outset South Africans have lacked a common identity and ideology. We were polarised for so long that there were sharp divisions, fractures even, which meant that uniting to build a nation may just have been too tall an order. Beyond the obvious racial differences and agendas, there was the economic divide, a chasm so deep that it seems impossible to bridge.

Nation-building requires practical integration of a society. How do you integrate a divided society where even the infrastructure was designed to keep people divided? We experienced a divided education system, separate living areas, separate health systems, even formal and informal economies based on race. There were few to no opportunities to bridge the gaps and exchange thoughts, ideas, and talents for the benefit of all parties. How could we think we would have a rainbow nation just because we willed it?

Goodwill is a start, of course, but there is significantly more required if South Africans are to overcome the internal colonialism that exists between us. The famous Irish author James Joyce said: 'A nation is the same people living in the same place.'[2] Only when South Africans accept that we are all the same people can we hope to start from the same foundation as we build our nation. We will not achieve true nation-building until we recognise that we need to intensify natural social exchanges among South Africans of different social and cultural backgrounds. Social cohesion can only come about when we find common ground among ourselves as South Africans.

The other side of nation-building involves building the state. Ideally, to do this, the two cornerstones of identity building and societal integration are needed to anchor the foundation. To build up the state from this foundation, we require more than a government; we need a functional government, a government recognising that it is representative of its constituents and that it must therefore respect the citizenry and protect everyone's human rights.

Nation-building also needs a firm and functional judiciary; the nation must be able to demonstrate its ability to protect its citizens. It must have a capable and efficient economy that seeks to uplift the status of all citizens, especially its poor and vulnerable. Infrastructure that attends to these social requirements stands the country in good stead for developing a healthy and harmonious society.

It is evident, then, that nation-building is a multi faceted endeavour, involving social, economic, and political sectors that must not be allowed to disintegrate or fail if the nation is to succeed. The danger in new democracies like ours is that they are susceptible to dictatorial or suppressive regimes, especially when political and economic elites use nation-building as a vehicle to drive their own agendas. US ex-president Jimmy Carter said: 'A strong nation, like a strong person, can afford to be gentle, firm, thoughtful, and restrained. It can afford to extend a helping hand to others. It's a weak nation, like a weak person, that must behave with bluster and boasting and rashness and other signs of insecurity.'[3]

We can never hope for a populace willing to engage with one another if one group of our people feels marginalised and ignored, another feels relegated to irrelevance, and yet other groups feel they never got the revolution they were hoping for. A common nationality is not a miracle of democracy; it's an objective we are working towards.

Currently the ANC has divisive policies that are the antithesis of nation-building, especially in business, and these divisive policies are filtering down into the social cracks of dissension and swelling with disharmony. We simply have to stop the ANC in its tracks before the cracks yield to the pressure and the edifice disintegrates under our very feet.

It is against this background of a shaky nation that I propose how business needs to transform, because economic transformation, in association with social and political reform, can help to mend some of the fractures that keep South Africans divided.

One of the policies most harmful to business is affirmative action. It not only prevents people being employed on merit—it cuts out 10% of our population from competing fairly to be employed. But worse than that, it fosters racism in the workplace and in social interactions. If the ANC leaders want to create a level economic playing field, then it is their responsibility to ensure that everyone has access to equal educational opportunities so that graduates are capable and confident of their ability to earn the job they desire. As soon as BEE stagnated, the government upgraded it to BBBEE—broad-based black economic empowerment. Adding letters to the alphabet soup of a discriminatory practice won't improve business; it just fuels already existing discontent. How can we hope for natural social integration if a sector of our populace feels excluded and dismissed?

If the government is serious about giving all businesses a fair bite at the apple of economic empowerment, then it must begin at the highest level and empower the Minister of Labour to use discretion in extending bargaining council agreements.

As the law currently stands, the minister is forced to extend bargaining council agreements to non-parties. This type of legislation prevents thousands and thousands of prospective business owners from entering the economy simply because they cannot afford to comply with limiting and onerous bargaining council agreements. The exclusion of these potential employers in turn excludes more than 50% of our youth from ever—ever—becoming employed. How can we hope to embark on healthy nation-building when such a significant chunk of our population has no hope of ever working?

The minimum-wage legislation precludes unskilled labour from ever knowing what it's like to be employed. By enforcing a minimum wage, the government has excluded unskilled workers from ever being employed. It cuts them off at the knees, and they will never be able to climb onto the ladder of employment. If the government had an ounce of compassion, it would allow people the freedom to negotiate what they are prepared to work for, so that they can become self-sufficient and improve their skills so as to work their way up to higher-paying positions. It is inhuman to prevent people from working.

Against this background, and from my own personal history, I know that the only way forward for impoverished and unemployed people in this country is for them to pull themselves out of poverty. It's a grim reality to face, but since the government currently exercises its brutal ignorance of our poor, the only solution is for poor people to empower themselves. And the only way existing businesses can survive is to lobby government to change the restrictive laws that frustrate us in becoming employers of the poor to alleviate the criminal level of poverty that exists. If business owners and entrepreneurs want to be competitive in the economy, then we must make strategic decisions about how best to circumvent labour laws that limit our participation in the economy.

Having briefly discussed the economic transformation that is necessary for nation-building, I would now like to focus on active citizenship as an important facet of nation-building, because it is only when every single one of us realises our civic responsibility that we can look towards robust nation-building and meaningful transformation. Kofi Annan said: 'Whether our challenge is peace-making, nation-building, democratization, or responding to natural or man-made disaster, we have seen that even the strongest amongst us cannot succeed alone.'[4] I would like to unpack the term 'active citizenship' so that we can start to conceptualise it, and implement it, instead of it just being a buzzword.

The South African Constitution contains the Bill of Rights that extends rights to all South African citizens. As citizens we are members of a community that shares the same rights, and we expect to be treated in the same way as everyone else in the community. Having equal rights extended to us suggests that we have a responsibility to uphold those rights, and thus it is inferred that active citizens are those who fulfil our rights and responsibilities in a balanced way.

By active citizenship I mean an individual's involvement

in public life and affairs. In a local context, this would refer to citizens involved in tackling problems or effecting change in our communities. These citizens develop knowledge, enabling informed decisions that will improve quality of life in these communities. On a national level, active citizenship includes campaigning to bring about change, protesting against poverty, and exercising voting rights. Active citizenship means being informed about public life, and developing knowledge, critical thinking, and independent judgement, and then using these skills to make decisions about our community or country and taking action either individually or collectively. Active citizens are entitled to challenge laws, rules, and existing structures within the democratic processes. As active citizens we must be open and tolerant; and we must respect justice, the rule of law, and democracy; and we must be willing to defend perspectives and listen to and stand up for others.

South Africa has a good track record of active citizenship that has roots in the demonstrations against apartheid and now continues in the form of service delivery protests and trade union strikes. Why then are we currently experiencing a wider community deficit in active citizenship? Why have many South Africans not embraced the notion of active citizenship?

Looking at the demographics of the country, we can acknowledge that we have a percentage of the population living in fairly remote rural areas, and we can understand that this population has not yet grasped the privilege of citizenship in a democratic country. But what about the indifferent attitudes of urban South

Africans? In spite of our democratic dispensation, indifference sets a dangerous precedent of the government working in isolation. What are some of the reasons for the indifference and passivity in citizens across the geographical and socio-economic spectrum?

Prior to 1994 the majority of South Africans were marginalised by government policies that undermined our human rights. Post-1994 the country experienced a transition from apartheid to a democracy, and a liberal one at that. This dramatic turnaround should have been accompanied with initiatives to educate communities about democratic processes and the benefits of citizenship accruing to these communities. Lack of such initiatives has resulted in many people in rural areas being uninformed about how to access government processes for participation, and thus they remain passive citizens. It is also possible that the subjugation of South Africans during apartheid has carried over into our democracy, resulting in communities continuing to look to the government to lead strategies of transformation and development—meaning communities are passive and in effect approve of the government acting in what officials believe to be communities' best interests.

Possibly through privilege, some South Africans believe that the hard-won democracy wasn't their fight and therefore feel they have no role to play in civic affairs. Yet if we all accept our rights as citizens and exercise our responsibilities accordingly, then we can hold the government accountable. Failure to be active citizens only widens the chasm between government and communities, keeping government organisations from purposely and accountably acting on citizens' concerns and demands. It also condones governmental dysfunction.

How do we overcome this apathy? To encourage active citizenship, we need to identify communities where there is a democratic deficit and educate citizens and public officials regarding the rights and responsibilities people have in a democracy. Only once people realise we all have an important role to play in developing local democratic structures will active citizenship be realised.

Some South Africans observe a preference for expansive acts of activism rather than active citizenry on a smaller scale, thinking that an impressive show will mean their voices will be heard. We must reject this tendency.

It is precisely because we have citizens who don't know how the process of active citizenship works that we experience violent service delivery protests leading to looting and arson and destruction of municipal properties. Some people don't seem to grasp that state property belongs to the citizens, and they are destroying the very facilities that should be serving them. If these frustrated communities understood the democratic process involved, they would realise that they do have agency, and that it is their right to contribute to government's decisions. Such active citizenship can take place through sharing frustrations, attending community meetings, joining forums, peaceful protest, signing petitions, and voting.

However, active citizenship should be concerned with more than just absorbing the protocols of engagement and learning how to participate within the existing models of interaction. It needs to embrace political literacy and empowerment and address relations of power. It needs to promote community solidarity and social cohesion, both to strengthen civil society and to empower individuals. Social inclusion is imperative.

Where do you stand on the active-citizen continuum?

Most of us are ordinary apathetic individuals who really are not concerned with playing a role in social affairs. However, once we are exposed to something that threatens our world, we may volunteer to get involved. As volunteers we may have good intentions to help, but we're not always sufficiently educated about the democratic processes required to address the social issues. If we are able to grow in understanding, we then become conscientious citizens. And we start asking why: why have we been promised water and why aren't we receiving it? We then become interested in discovering the causes of the problems and are propelled into action, leading us to become active citizens for whom our community becomes a priority in our values and life choices.

Critics of active citizenship argue that public consultation does not achieve anything and that citizens grow increasingly disinclined to engage on issues that matter to them. Some citizens believe opportunities for engagement are no more than gestures of inclusion, and nothing will result from their engagement. Some feel there is merely a façade of engagement—that issues have already been decided, and that their participation cannot effect change. If we are serious about encouraging active citizenship, we have to be careful how we frame the opportunity for dialogue, and how the interaction is managed, and we need to ensure that there is report-back on the outcomes of these interactions. People who are civically minded generally want to participate in conversations that will result in real and meaningful impact.

A two-year UK research study showed that when active citizens experience a combination of an empowering quality experience and a resourceful activist environment, then participation continues; but when they have poor-quality experiences, or the environment is hostile, or they experience a serious life event, their participation in active citizenship ends.

To ensure that our active citizenship is a rewarding experience, we must accept that our opinion is the way we view and think about the world and that this viewpoint may not necessarily be reflective of other people's perspectives. To foster tolerance of differing viewpoints, we must debate our differences so that we can find solutions agreeable to all. We must consider all sides of an argument as well as other people's opinions so that we can make informed decisions, instead of emotional ones. Communication is key to ensuring that our perceptions are clearly conveyed, and tolerance is key to understanding and being understood.

We must recognise that not everyone is capable of the same level of active citizenship. There is formal active citizenship and informal active citizenship. On the informal side we have individual actions, such as making donations or making certain consumer choices. Then we have community actions, such as participating in the neighbourhood watch or community policing forum or taking part in protest action. In formal active citizenship, individuals can attend meetings, sign petitions, volunteer, or vote. Collectively, these individuals can campaign and lobby, join a governing body, become a trustee, stand for local elections, or forge relationships with decision-makers. There is no one-size-fits-all model of active citizenship. Active citizenship simply requires that people get involved, that they play an active role in their community, at their workplace, in a political organisation, or at a protest rally. The activity itself is not the main issue; what is important is the individual's commitment to building a healthy society.

It is not the ground beneath our feet that creates South Africa; it is the people who walk on that ground and make up her citizenry. As active citizens we must demand a representative government that respects human rights and protects the rights of its citizens. To achieve the social cohesion that nation-building seeks, especially in a culturally diverse country, we simply must see it develop from within our society, from finding commonality among ourselves.

CHAPTER 13

SUPPORTING ONE ANOTHER

A s I was finishing this book my friends Daisy and Seggy Govender introduced me to the Naicker family at a social gathering. Conversation turned to some of the topics I was addressing, and I told them I wanted to incorporate an example of how harmonious relations can be in South Africa, because I believe we all have it in us to reach out to one another. Daisy insisted that the Naicker family tell me their story. As the story unfolded, I realised our meeting was made to order.

Needing domestic help, the Naickers hired a young woman they barely knew. To protect her privacy I'll call her TC (for her birth order as the third child). In her they found willing effort and hard work. Needing further education, the young woman told them of her hopes. And in her new employers she found protagonists. Their joint experience portrays what thoughtfulness and decency can accomplish. Together TC and the Naickers have built things that were not there before—confidence, surefootedness, a new career, love. Here is their story, in their own words.

TC: I have four brothers, and I'm the third child in the family. My father stopped working in 1984 when I was born because he had asthma and the doctors said he couldn't work anymore. He resigned, but he continued working in the construction industry, because he was the only one supporting our family. By the time I reached high school, his health deteriorated and he went on pension, which kept us going for a while. My mom was a housewife; she has never worked. My parents wanted to ensure that we were all educated, so they sent us all to school.

My mother never had the opportunity to go to school, but her older brother did attend school and whenever he returned home at the end of the school day, my mother insisted that he teach her whatever he had learned. So, before we even started school, my mom taught us how to read and write. Sometimes she'd take me outside and she would teach me to write in the sand, and teach me to count with stones because we didn't have a calculator or counters. She was resourceful. She doesn't understand English, so she taught us in Zulu. I was well prepared for my first year at school, because whatever the teacher taught us, I already knew because my mom used my brother's books as a guide to teach me.

When I matriculated, I was determined to help my family. When I finished school a job was my main priority. But a matric certificate is just a piece of paper; it doesn't take you anywhere. I wanted to further my studies, but it wasn't an option in our house because my parents couldn't afford it. After weeks of job hunting, I became despondent and thought I would never find a good job, so I changed my attitude and I just started looking for any job.

I managed to find a job at a factory that made T-shirts. I earned about a R150 a week, for a full week's work. On Thursdays I worked a 24-hour shift from morning right throughout the night, and then I was off on Friday. I tried to save R50 and use the R100 for basic necessities, but R100 wasn't enough to live on, so I never managed to save anything.

When that job ended I went from door to door on the KwaZulu-Natal South Coast looking for a domestic job. Sometimes I would get a piece job, but they were very unsatisfactory and I thought: this isn't how things should be.

I once applied for a domestic position, and the employer was pleasant and explained that they would register me if I brought my identity document. When explaining my duties, they said I must wait at the gate to be let in and out of the property, that I would have my own cutlery and crockery, and I was expected to take my meals outside. I was shown how to carry certain items. They were friendly but I was really uncomfortable, and I thought if this was how they were treating me on the first day, I couldn't see myself lasting. I felt it was wrong to treat someone the way they treated me. I never went back.

In 2002 I came to Durban and I was prepared to take any job. I started working for a friend of Marlynee and worked there for about three years until she emigrated. In 2005 I found a job at a carwash. My English was not fluent, and I knew the reason I didn't have much confidence in job hunting was because I didn't feel confident communicating. I tried to get my hands on as many books as I could to read and teach myself to improve my language skills. I tried to socialise more with people who spoke good English and tried to improve my vocabulary and proficiency. Even if people didn't always understand me, I persevered. I kept on reading and talking and practising. I earned R20 a day and it was a take-it-or-leave-it situation, so I accepted the low salary. I noticed that my employer spoke to and about the other employees with no respect. However, when she saw me approaching, her demeanour changed because she knew I understood what she was saying. I believe I was treated better than other employees because of my English fluency.

My employer also owned a crèche, and she said, 'I don't want you to work in the carwash anymore, I want you to work at the crèche, because I can see that you can communicate with people.' I was excited, and I took the job. Although the job entailed more responsibility, it didn't mean that I would earn more and I was disappointed.

I worked at the crèche from Monday to Friday, but to supplement my salary, to earn a bit more, I asked if I could also work at the carwash on the weekends, and the owner agreed. I managed to earn a bit extra, but I didn't earn any tips because I wasn't a carwash celebrity like the regulars who knew their customers.

I'd been working at the crèche for a while when Marlynee's friend who had emigrated came to Durban for a visit. She left a voice message saying she had found my number on an old telephone bill: 'I just hope this is TC—please call me back if it's you.' When I phoned her, she told me Marlynee was looking for somebody to help her, and that I might be interested. I said I would like to meet the family, but I didn't leave the carwash then because the deal wasn't sealed.

Marlynee Naicker: It was quite by chance that TC came into our lives. Our long-serving domestic worker, Paulina, had a growing family of her own and her husband decided she should return home to look after them, which was understandable. My daughter Saihini was six years old, and my son Daiyin was three months old, and I wondered how I was going to manage a full-time job and look after two young children. A friend visiting from the UK mentioned that she knew someone who might fit the bill and gave me TC's telephone number, saying she wasn't quite sure if I could still reach TC on that number, that the contact number might be outdated, but that I should try anyway. My husband Asogan and I arranged to meet TC on the roadside in Claire Estate, near to where TC was working.

TC: We arranged to meet after work, and Asogan and Marlynee came to where I was working in Claire Estate. Daiyin was about three months old and I was intimidated by this tiny baby. Asogan and Marlynee briefed me on what they were looking for in a helper and what duties were expected of me. I told them what I could do for them, and they asked to meet me on the weekend to negotiate further.

They fetched me on the weekend and we had lunch together, and they told me what they needed. I had worked in a lot of places by then—in a factory, in a carwash, in various domestic piece jobs, and at the crèche. I had always taken on almost any job that I could get because I wanted to save money for my studies; I knew my parents couldn't afford to pay for the fees. But when I met Marlynee and Asogan I knew that I wanted to work for them because of how they conducted the interview.

Marlynee: One never knows how things are going to work out. TC arrived and we explained to her that, since she would be taking care of our children, we expected her to assimilate herself into our lives. If she was hungry or thirsty then she was to help herself to what she wanted, and when we were at home at mealtimes, she was expected to join us. Basically, we wanted her to feel as though she was a member of the family.

TC: When I arrived at their home in Durban, Asogan and Marlynee showed me around and settled me in my room. They invited me to eat meals with them, and told me that I was free to relax in my room, watch TV, or shower whenever I wanted to. It came as a shock because I was used to former employers handing me dirty blankets. Everything in the Naicker home was clean and appropriate. The fact that they gave me a bunch of keys on the day I walked in and said, 'Here are your keys, because we're in and out all the time, and you are welcome to come and go as you please' was an amazing realisation that these people trusted me.

Marlynee told me to relax and that she would show me what to do. But the next day, she didn't show me anything. I panicked and thought, 'I came here to work, but she's not showing me anything!' I decided I had to just get up and work and do whatever I thought was best. You know when you get a job and you want it to work out, but you have to prove yourself? The overriding challenge for me was to look after the children well. I thought I had to make sure that Daiyin didn't cry—I was afraid of what they would think if the baby was crying in my care. I tried so hard to keep him calm.

Those first few days were really scary. I was still expecting them to treat me in the same way other employers had treated me: 'You can't do this, you can't touch that. Ask for permission to do things.' I didn't have to call Asogan and Marlynee Mr and Mrs. It was never boss and madam; it was never that. But I soon managed to relax, because I realised that Marlynee and Asogan weren't watching my every move, that I was free to live freely. If Marlynee came home and Daiyin was crying, she didn't blame me for his tears. She realised babies cry and that it wasn't a reflection on me. She didn't check up to see if I'd dusted here, or cleaned there. I didn't feel watched. But then also because they were so natural and normal, I didn't want to take advantage of them.

I appreciated that they treated me well, and I didn't want to spoil that. I knew I wouldn't find it again. Even when it came to salary negotiation, instead of telling me what they expected of me, they explained how my salary would work. Asogan sat down and explained that when I was due for a salary increase of 4% this was how it would work. They had a trusting relationship with me. I knew that I could count on them, so why spoil that?

Finally, I realised my dream of being able to save, because, in addition to my salary, they provided accommodation, food, transport savings, and a weekend off. I was saving in a post office account that I had. Previously I used to work and save a little, and then I'd be unemployed and have to use those savings to sustain myself. Asogan explained that I would earn a better rate of interest if I opened a bank account, so they helped me to open a bank account and paid my salary into it. Money never really seems to be enough, but whatever you do earn, you can budget around it. I still had my dreams, but I no longer had many expenses, so I could save.

Marlynee: I was on maternity leave at the time, and I realised right away that TC was fantastic with the children and that she coped well with them. I returned to work and TC was so proactive in her duties. I'd return home and the vegetables and meat would be prepared, ready for me to cook, or she'd take the initiative and make a meal for the family—she makes an excellent cottage pie.

When Daiyin turned two, we sent him to Montpelier School situated a block away. TC was fabulous. We would come home and TC would be sitting at the table with Daiyin on her lap, doing homework with Saihini. We had never asked TC to do so, nor expected it of her, but you could really see how much she involved herself in the lives of the children.

Asogan Naicker: One day when we came home, I said, 'TC, you shouldn't be doing domestic duties. You need to be studying to keep your mind active.' I asked TC if she had the opportunity to study, what she would choose. She was taken aback.

TC: I was so surprised when Asogan asked me what I wanted to study. I had never shared my dreams with him or Marlynee because I respected them as my employers, and I still do. As much as they had been receptive of me, I am very reserved, and I don't share much. I don't even think I told them I was saving because I wanted to study further! Although I didn't really understand what food technology meant, it appealed to me.

Marlynee: TC started researching and said she wanted to study food technology. We suggested that, since she clearly had a talent for child care, she should consider something in that field.

TC: When Asogan and Marlynee offered to assist me to further my studies, I was surprised. I didn't know what had motivated them to ask me.

Asogan: I always say I had the privilege of growing up poor, and I use the term loosely, but I mean it. My father never had a job for more than a year. He was a labourer, and we were poor. My mom was a housewife who raised five children. We battle to raise two children—I don't know how they managed with five children and no resources, but they did. I could never say that I was an unhappy child; we were always content with what we had and made do with our meagre resources. If we lost everything, I'd survive. I can go barefoot on the street again and I'd make it.

I think my impoverished childhood was a privilege because I can identify with society at large, and some people can't, especially those who were born with a silver spoon in their mouths.

They don't know otherwise. It's a privilege that I've been exposed to poor conditions. I wouldn't want it any other way, because it shaped me as a person. Coming from such a background made me humble. I don't have the arrogance of being born rich and privileged. So I actually mean it when I say I was privileged to have been born into those circumstances.

TC, I realised, had so much potential, and even though empowering her meant that we would lose her as our housekeeper, it didn't feel right to watch that potential go to waste.

TC: When Marlynee said, 'You're very good with children,' I thought maybe there was something I wasn't seeing. And when I gave it some thought I realised that the crèche owner must also have recognised my ability to work with children, even though I really hadn't considered it. I was still hung up on food technology and made inquiries, but the course I investigated was full-time study and that wasn't a possibility.

Marlynee suggested teaching, and she did some research and mentioned the correspondence college. She showed me the brochures and suggested I enquire there and see how it went. They offered an Early Childhood Development course, so I went there, and they advised me about the fees and everything, and they said, 'Well, you're in!' And Marlynee sorted everything out for me.

Marlynee: TC enrolled in a one-year diploma course in child development. The college advised that TC could study towards three years of certificates and then go to UNISA, and that with all her qualifications she could do a BTech. The principal at

Montpelier suggested that TC should rather enrol for a Bachelor of Education through UNISA, but since we had already paid for the courses at the correspondence college, TC decided to complete the certificate courses.

TC: I hadn't known what to expect. I had never imagined myself working and studying at the same time, so I knew that was going to be a challenge. I had to try to work out a plan as to how I was going to manage everything. I wanted to prove this to myself. I kept saying, 'I really want this and I can do it.' I really wanted to show Marlynee and Asogan that their faith wasn't misplaced in giving me this opportunity. The reason I took on the correspondence course was because I didn't have to attend classes and I would be working at the Naicker home, so part-time study suited my schedule.

When I started I was computer illiterate, and Saihini really helped me a lot. I was allowed to use the computer and I wasn't limited on the internet. The Naickers provided all the resources and support I needed. Whenever I needed help, I just had to ask. If I had to make copies, then Asogan would say, 'Don't worry, I'll take it to the office and make copies for you.' I would be shy if I needed 30 copies, but nothing was too much for them. If I needed to send things, they would email them for me. They were so helpful. I remember one time thinking that this moment had been waiting for me all my life—I just had to struggle a little, and then the opportunity opened up for me. They helped me with almost everything. Sometimes, I would ask Saihini for help, and she'd try to help me. Sometimes she was wrong, but she always tried to help me figure things out and we would get it right. Sometimes Asogan would come across us working on something, and he would immediately sit down and help us.

When I submitted my first assignment and it was returned with an 80% mark, I immediately phoned Asogan and Marlynee; I was so excited. They took me out to celebrate. I got to choose the restaurant, and they said, 'Have whatever you want TC, this is your moment.' It was a different reaction to what would have happened at home. If I had told my mom, there's no doubt that she would have been happy, but she wasn't in a position to celebrate my achievement. It made me mindful that my mom would have loved to do what I was doing, but she never had the opportunity. I realised I had found myself other parents who had anchored me and nurtured me.

The course was assignment-based without exams, so there was never that exam pressure. However, during the second year, we had to do a practical component and be involved with the children, so I went to a school where I met another lady who said she was doing the same course through UNISA, but it was a degree course. I thought: that's what I need, because I won't go far with a certificate.

Marlynee: We again consulted the principal at Montpelier, Gail King, and explained that TC was interested in doing something along the lines of child development and had enrolled at a cor-respondence college, where we were told she could get recog-nition for her certificates at UNISA and complete a BTech. Gail told us this advice was nonsense and that the right way to go was indeed for TC to be doing a Bachelor of Education through UNISA.

TC: I was afraid to approach Marlynee and Asogan about the opportunity at UNISA, and I spent days thinking about how best to approach the subject. But I needn't have worried, because when I told them I would like to take the degree course at UNISA, they said, 'If it's recognised, and it will improve your chances, then find out about it.' So during my second year of study at the correspondence school, I started the degree course through UNISA.

My life changed. I was studying two courses and doing the housework and looking after the baby. I'm not the type of person who writes down her plans. I have a plan in my head, and I always have Plan B. I avoid writing things down, because then I feel compelled to follow them through, and I don't want pressure to get in the way of being flexible. I always believe that if Plan A doesn't work, then Plan B will work. So that's how I moved forward. UNISA was far more pressure. There were due dates, textbooks required, and exams. And I was looking after a demanding Daiyin, who tugged at my dress if I didn't give him the attention he deserved. So I had to juggle how I was going to keep him occupied, do the housework, and study. I would feed him and settle him down in front of the TV and put on a DVD. I tried to get through the housework so that by midday I could sit down with him and do what he wanted to do. I was able to give him time as well. Then I would go to my room in the evenings and do my studying. I would study until about 10.00 pm and during exam times I would wake up at 3.00 am. It worked well for me. Study until 6.00, shower, go inside at 6.30, prepare breakfast and the children's lunches, and get ready myself, and go to school on the days I had practicals. When I finished at 12.30 I would start my housekeeping and child-care chores at 1.00 pm and juggle Daiyin and work. He just wanted to play soccer—he didn't understand my needs. I tried to work out a routine with him: eat, go to sleep, play, and that routine helped me to get through everything. Teaching him the routine made managing my life easier. He would wake up and come to my room where I was ironing, and if I didn't have any other work to do I would take him and play or do whatever he wanted to do.

I did feel overwhelmed, because although I tried to stick to a schedule as much as possible, sometimes the workload was heavy and I felt pressurised. I was afraid that Marlynee and Asogan would think now that I was studying, I wasn't getting their work done, and I wouldn't look after the children properly. Although I felt the pressure I didn't share it with anyone. I just reminded myself that this is life and I won't sulk; there's no solution. I am working and studying. But each year got more challenging. By my third or fourth year, I approached Marlynee and Asogan and explained that the workload had increased, and that the children were getting older, there was homework, and with my own workload of studying, I wasn't coping. I said it would be better if I got somebody to share the load; if somebody could at least do half of my household chores, I would feel better able to cope. I explained that I would still always be there for the children. The family was very understanding.

Marlynee: TC would study, go to school for her practicals, then come home at midday and clean and look after the children. In terms of affordability we couldn't afford two helpers.

TC: Asogan explained that if we took on another helper, my salary would have to be cut, which was understandable. As long as I could pull through, it was a solution that could work for me. We found a lady to come in the mornings and help while I was at school, and it worked very well.

It was only when I reached fourth year at UNISA, that I could finally see a path in front of me. It was different from working at the carwash. At the carwash, you can't look at a car and say, 'I want that car.' You can like the car, but you don't bother desiring it, because it's not going to happen. You touch it, but you know you'll never have it. But now I had been given an opportunity, and I had been given the ability to dream, and I could see the possibility of my dream coming true. It's empowering. In my final year of studying, I could finally see myself being a teacher. Saihini asks me what it feels like to be a teacher, and I don't really know what to say.

Marlynee: In 2014 TC graduated with a distinction. Her dad attended the graduation ceremony. It was a proud moment for all of us.

TC: Now that I'm teaching I see the challenges in education and I feel small. I guess you never are where you want to be. When I'm teaching, I am trying to improve those children's lives, but the senior staff who aren't involved with children insist upon what strategies have to be implemented. My suggestions fall on deaf ears. There is no room for creative solutions and it is frustrating. I get comments like, 'I did it like this in 1976', so you have to do it that way too. But this isn't 1976. My frustration makes me think I should study further and get a job at the education department and tell them that their strategies aren't working, that they aren't useful. I want to say, 'You're just destroying the future of these children with these outdated ways.'

I feel that the education system is devastating because it is limiting. The strategies are designed by maybe two people who wrote the book and have their own method of how it should be taught. But when I refer to the textbook, the children don't understand the content; it's not at their level. When I make worksheets to suit the learners' levels, the senior staff reprimand me about wasting resources. The senior staff want things done their way, and they don't want it changed.

I also think there needs to be an empowerment programme for parents, because most of the parents are uneducated and don't seem to understand educational processes or the importance of being involved in their children's lives. Many parents only return home from work at about 8.00 pm in the evening, or else the learners' grandmother caregivers can't read. I no longer give homework because it never gets done. Parents view homework as teachers shirking their responsibilities. They don't realise education is a partnership, and that homework is just reinforcement of the lessons' concepts. Sometimes I call the parents to discuss their child so that I can understand what is going on at home in order to help the child. I'm willing to spend an extra hour or so a day to help these learners, and then the parents say 'do whatever you have to do', but they will never come and follow up to see if their child is improving. They don't even read the term reports, which are always sent back unsigned.

I try as far as possible to help where I can. I take in extra resources of my own to encourage the learners. Rather than follow the senior staff's strategies, I close the classroom door and do my own thing in the classroom, because I don't want my seniors to see what we're doing. It might appear to them that we're just playing, but we're learning, and I know the results of these activities; I know that we are learning. I try to get the learners to work diligently during the week, and then on Fridays we'll have a quiz to test the week's learning content; it helps me to see if the content has been learned and it reinforces learning. One morning the principal came in, didn't see any files or work on the learners' desks, and said, 'I'm very disappointed. Nobody's doing any work, or reading; you're just sitting.' I explained that we were working, but she explained that other staff might think I'm not doing my job. I don't get support.

My fellow teachers feel the same way. I think perhaps my experience during my teaching practice at a private school has given me different expectations. I haven't made friends at work; work is strictly work. I'm there to teach. No social interaction, just professional. We joke, but we're not friends. I ask them if they're scared of being fired if we voice our opinions. They say other schools aren't like ours, and if we can survive at this school we can survive anywhere. There is a teacher who has been there for 21 years, but she shows no initiative. Although I privately question, I try not to say too much. When I have a problem I approach my supervisor; if she doesn't help, I'll go to someone else.

The department has a rule that if the child is physically too big, you can't fail them. This is so dangerous. This is the foundation stage. If you push them ahead without skills at this stage, what kind of uneducated adults will they become? I feel frustrated. My teachers produced a diligent student in me. What am I going to produce by pushing children through grades when they don't have the basic concepts, the foundation concepts for the rest of their education? Will I produce the alcoholics, the drug addicts and non-conformists? The social behaviour of some learners is shocking, and yet when you talk to the parents, very often the parents are also depressed and lost. Although I try my very best, I realise I've only got a year with them, and the school system's approach is just destroying them. That's why I want to study further and help to make positive changes in teaching.

Some learners think that the disciplinary rules only apply at school, and at home they're exposed to fighting, drinking, and smoking, so they think that's what life is. They conform to whatever environment they find themselves in. At home they behave badly, and at school they behave well. They don't feel like they're doing it for themselves—they feel like they're doing it for the teacher. They don't seem to realise that it's their own lives, that they're in charge of their lives, and what they do affects their lives. I think society is in trouble.

They come from disadvantaged homes so they don't mind stealing if they're hungry, so I teach them to share, which is alien to them. They're very used to worrying only about themselves. The level of violence is quite alarming. I have to teach them not to scream or lash out if someone stands on their foot by mistake. Parents can't be bothered with discipline because as far as they're concerned it's the school's duty to instil discipline; they don't realise it's a partnership between parent and teacher.

A child came to school with measles and I asked her if her mother saw her, but she said no, her mother was sleeping, but insisted she go to school and that the teacher would sort the child out. Some parents regard schools as babysitters. I phoned the mother and she came to school. I explained measles was contagious. She pretended it was less serious. They don't take any responsibility. I believe it's got to do with their age—90% of my learners have young parents. When I calculate their ages, most of them were teenage parents. They didn't finish school. Most of them don't even consider going back to school.

The KwaZulu-Natal education department employs me and I'm on probation for a year. Once I have stability, and I've got a future income stream, then I will start studying again. For now my focus is on stability and experience. If these are department rules, it's sad, because in four or five years' time, we won't have any generations who are interested in education. It's scary. There are children in Grade 7 who are incapable of writing a paragraph. It's sad. I have a colleague who teaches in high school, and he won't be returning to teaching next year because instead of attending classes, his learners go and smoke dagga on the playground and then come into class late. I think it's a social problem.

I have 51 children in my class. It's too many to manage effectively, but the headmistress says some schools have 120 in a class, and we say but this isn't another school—this is our school. We have to do group work that doesn't facilitate learning, because ideally a group should be a maximum of eight, and I have groups of 15. It doesn't work. Our classroom is so crowded. If you call them to the carpet there isn't room to accommodate them; you can't supervise 51 children efficiently. There is the internship programme whereby the department offers interns to assist teachers. When I inquired about it, I was told we have to apply to a government agency and it's too much bureaucracy. There's a protocol you have to follow. We have to submit our budget, but the government won't send staff to cope with the amount of learners we have. I usually ask the parents' permission to keep the weaker children for half an hour after school so that I can help them, even though we aren't really allowed to because of crime and transport issues, so often I have to let them go. I feel frustrated and limited because when you question whether it's government regulation or school regulation, you don't really get a straight answer.

Asogan and Marlynee empowered me. There aren't many people about to do that. They have had such a positive influence on my life, and I want to show my appreciation and thanks as much as I can. I think maybe the best way to do so is to help somebody in as much need as I was. I was given the opportunities, and the support, and I turned out well. I'd like to do that for somebody else. I didn't only receive an education—I received so much more, and most important, I know I've grown as a person. That's taught me a lot.

I love the family because they've been consistent from day one. They treat me as an equal; they've never made me feel inferior. I realise you cannot typecast people. Racism always comes up in discussions when I mention the Naickers. I always defend them. People generalise and say, 'Indians aren't nice,' and I say 'Not my people.' But racism is always there. It's difficult to break down stereotypes. I don't go all out to get involved in a debate, but I make sure people know that racism is not my experience. When I graduated, my father was so proud that he told everyone, but he doesn't know how to respond to Marlynee and Asogan. My mom thinks about them a lot, and she appreciates that they have been a surrogate family to me, but she's shy and doesn't know how to thank them. I hope that living up to what Marlynee and Asogan hoped for me is gratitude enough. I still rely on them for decisions. They are always there for me.

I can't believe how I've grown in confidence. I don't know how I did it. I think it was the faith they placed in me. They brought out the person in me that I didn't know existed.

I don't know if they see me as their child. Although they have absorbed me into the family, and treated me as one of their own, I'm afraid of crossing that boundary, because I don't want to spoil the relationship. What they have given me goes beyond words. Because of them I can dream further and I'm able to see the future, I'm able to see where I want to go.

Marlynee: TC lives with my mom-in-law in Durban, and she still comes to visit on the weekends and she spends family holidays with us. TC has become our eldest child. Before Asogan and I had Saihini and Daiyin, we discussed adopting an underprivileged child. Then when TC came into our lives and we witnessed the remarkable bond she shared with Saihini and Daiyin, I believed that this must be part of God's plan. I believe that some things in life are meant to be, and our paths crossing was the hand of fate.

Asogan: TC was a shy young lady who has blossomed into a soaring, self-confident, courageous woman, who is now able to express her feelings and opinions with conviction. She is such a special child, with a good heart. We have grown to love her dearly and wish only the best for her. We have rooted her and now she has wings to reach the heights of her potential.

*

TC took control of her life. She knew life was not fair, but she navigated it to her advantage. She never carried the misguided notion that the world owed her something or that the government was responsible for her well-being. Her story highlights the importance of allowing people to make their own decisions in the employment environment. People need to be able to decide for themselves what is a good job or not, and they need the freedom to move when it is time to move.

It hurts me deeply to see so many people unemployed, and yet the government keeps passing one law after another, claiming to be protecting people from exploitation. Given the space to apply their minds, people can work out for themselves what is good for them. And politicians in our country have proven beyond reasonable doubt that most are more interested in their personal agendas than in the public good.

TC and the Naicker family exemplify what South Africa can and should be. We have some worthy employers in this country; these are the people on whom we should focus our energy, and never mind the rhetoric about people being exploited. When you feel exploited or abused, move on. Why work for someone who is exploiting you? In a society of vigilant and conscious citizens, bad employers cannot get away with abuse. They will never have stability or continuity in their businesses because employees are mobile. The best weapons for government to use in protecting citizens are to educate them, create a full employment environment, and apply the rule of law.

The story of TC and the Naickers represents positive thinking, perseverance, hard work, a willingness to adapt, taking control of one's life, the good nature of human beings, and the danger of blanket racism.

CHAPTER 14

TRANSPARENCY SUSTAINS DEMOCRACY

When I was growing up I blamed white people and previous generations for my situation. I felt that others, from village chiefs to colonial powers, had determined our fate and destiny. I grew up failing to understand why my parents, family, community, and society at large were just content to carry on their daily lives without challenging their unacceptable living conditions. Perhaps this apathy had to do with the vicious manner in which the white powers dealt with their resistance.

Today South Africans are blaming everyone from Jan van Riebeeck to Jacob Zuma for the diabolical state of the nation. Albeit temporarily soothing, blaming others is an impractical strategy. Blame is an emotional response that prevents us from seeing things as they are. South Africa's history has not been documented in a collective way. When the National Party was in power, we were forced to swallow history that systematically showed black people in a negative light. Now we see a black push to obliterate white historical figures and 'decolonise' the political landscape. Such exclusivity only enforces divisiveness.

Blame destroys relationships because we become defensive. Blame prevents us from accepting responsibility; we yield to bitterness and despair, and we end up accepting the status quo. But most important, blame prevents us from learning. If we feel that we are not to blame for a situation, then we feel justified in not doing anything differently—leaving us in a perpetual cycle of apathy and anger. We are drowning in negativity. If on the other hand we forget blame and instead choose to engage with our particular reality, we can start developing a mindset more inclined towards problem-solving—towards the progressive solutions that are precisely what our country most needs. The presidency and leadership of Nelson Mandela embodied that kind of mindset. Coming out of a hostile prison after 27 years, he demonstrated practically the power and advantage of forward thinking and future-focused political tolerance. In the process, he won the hearts and minds of the entire global community, and the economy of the country supported him.

South Africa is today a democratic country, and we have the responsibility of shaping a different future. That future can only be shaped by acknowledging and incorporating the events and figureheads that make up our collective history, whether we agree or disagree with them, whether we like or dislike them. Consider Oxford University in England, or the Taj Mahal in India: such settings and monuments are part of the lasting physical record of a people's history. Concrete entities illustrate the lives of nations across centuries. Remembering our history is not to say that we must choke on the mud of negative deeds and tyrants. Rather, we need to stitch up the gaps; where gaps exist in history, discontent festers in those spaces. It is through a well-digested past that we can understand, forgive, learn, and move forward. Consider Japan and Germany: both lay in ruins after World War II, just 70 years ago, yet today both are beacons of economic strength.

It takes effort to see history this way. The Eurocentric perspectives we inherit are all about how colonialists enlightened Africa with civilisation and modern ways, while African scholars are keen to portray how colonialism plundered Africa and enslaved Africans, taking our land and depriving us of our human rights. I accept and believe both versions; each has its own truths. But there is no benefit in holding either responsible for how we go forward. We are all South Africans seeking a common purpose—a nation where we can all enjoy living and working.

Blame is not the same thing as accountability. It is perfectly acceptable to say that we hold the apartheid government responsible for destroying black society, and it is also perfectly acceptable to say that the ANC is ruining the South African economy and needs to be held accountable. Blame is an apathetic gesture, whereas demanding accountability is a proactive stance. Accountability is one of the pillars of governance in democratic countries. We now need to guard against the erosion of accountability and insist on extending it into our present and future, to avoid setting ourselves up for the kind of demise several African nations have suffered in recent decades. And to this end, we need to recognise that the other pillar of governance is transparency.

A democracy is not born overnight. It cannot be willed into being. The transition to democracy demands democratisation of institutions, systems, and processes within a country to achieve a lasting democratic state. Accountability and transparency are two key tools in that project.

We have a lot to lose. As post-1994 South Africa sought to counteract the poor governance of the autocratic apartheid regime, we facilitated our transition to democracy by establishing accountable and stable institutions, among them the National Director of Public Prosecutions, the Auditor-General, the Judicial Service Commission, the Human Rights Commission, and the Constitutional Court. However, when Zuma as the leader of the ANC states that the ANC is 'more important than the Constitution', we have cause for concern.[1] South Africa may have the appropriate democratic structures in place, but we seem to have reached a situation where these institutions have been so fully penetrated by the ANC majority that its control of the civil service has made it a dominant regime. Top positions in the civil service are filled by ANC supporters, making it almost impossible to establish an independent civil service. We may have a functioning democracy, but its functionality will not be sustainable if it continues on this trajectory, and unfortunately the economy will be the greatest casualty. As a capitalist—as someone who strongly believes in the free-market economic system—my most pressing concern therefore is to encourage South Africans to demand accountability and transparency.

The Constitution insists upon transparency in government actions and guarantees citizens' rights to information. By voting, we have assigned our power to our chosen delegates; this power should be wielded in accordance with the Constitution, and if it is not, the public officials should be held accountable. Transparency ensures that we as citizens have the right to information we can use to measure public officials' performance. To this end, transparency supports accountability. Without transparency and accountability, a relationship of trust between a government and its citizens is impossible. Where there is no trust, it is impossible to establish social stability and confidence in a country, both of which are needed to foster an environment favourable for economic growth.

In democratic societies the media are a key institution for facilitating government accountability. Media freedom is a necessary element in an accountable democracy, especially in a country where we have one dominant political party. A free media provides the public with reliable and accurate news and supports the democratic process, instead of the media serving as a political mouthpiece for one party. Among the democratic structures that were established post-1994 was the freedom of information. Today, I am concerned with the threats the media are facing. Some of the largest media houses in the country are now owned and operated by ANC supporters, and several prominent journalists have unashamedly revealed their political allegiance to the ANC. Political control of the media and the suppression of information are forces that every citizen should view with concern. Government-controlled media collude with the government and prevent it being transparent and accountable. Independent media are essential. In April 2015 Communications Minister Faith Muthambi reiterated the government's quest to regulate and transform the South African media. The last thing our democratic country needs is such political regulation. We need a more brutal and fearless press.

The Secrecy Bill, which threatens the press freedom enshrined in the Constitution, is a move the presidency has been sitting on for almost two years at the time of writing. It would criminalise investigative journalists, whistleblowers, and civil society activists who use freedom of information and expression to expose government shenanigans. Investigative journalism will fall under the Secrecy Bill's broad definition of espionage and will carry a penalty of up to 25 years in jail. Enactment of this legislation will result in government-controlled media no better than in North Korea or Syria or Burma. Transparency and accountability will go up in smoke. If we think we're in the dark now about government underhandedness and corruption, we will be even more so. To maintain the transparency and accountability essential to democracy, we have to protest vociferously against the Secrecy Bill and other actions suppressing media freedom.

Without transparency, we can forget about effective

government. Transparency is key to the efficiency of public policy. Public scrutiny is a known deterrent to reckless expenditure. Moreover, the IMF has identified a significant correlation between transparency and control of corruption. Worldwide Governance Indicators shows that South Africa has slid down the control-of-corruption scale from 80% in 1996 to 55% in 2013.[2] A major aspect of corruption is economic rent-seeking, whereby corrupt bureaucrats solicit bribes (rent) for using their authority to award benefits to others. A case in point is the recently uncovered FIFA 2010 scandal, in which bribes are suspected to have been paid to secure the World Cup hosting rights. Trade restrictions are another example of government-induced rents. Trade constraints create quantitative restrictions, whereas an open economy cuts out the situations where bribery and corruption can flourish. Government subsidies and incentives are another potential breeding ground for corruption to thrive, since subsidies and incentives are often misappropriated by unintended beneficiaries through bribery and corruption. Low wages in the civil service, such as in the metropolitan police departments, are a source of low-level corruption: public employees feel underpaid and use their positions of power to elicit bribes. Countries rich in mineral resources are often more vulnerable to rent-seeking than countries with low mineral resources, because the industries are heavily regulated and corrupt officials facilitate corrupt deals. In South Africa we also see social factors contributing to rent-seeking, as when public officials favour their relatives or tribal brothers.

Corruption is negatively linked to economic growth. According to the IMF: 'If the corruption index improves by one standard deviation ... the investment rate increases by more than 4 percentage points and the annual growth rate of per capita GDP increases by over a half percentage point. In effect, a country that improves its standing on the corruption index from, say, 6 to 8 (recall that 0 is most corrupt, 10 least), will enjoy the benefits of an increase of 4 percentage points of investment, with consequent improvement in employment and economic growth.'[3] That is, curbing corruption increases the employment rate. To realise such investment benefits, South Africa has to increase transparency and accountability to transform the areas in which corruption is flourishing.

Countering corruption requires building integrity. According to author Satishchander Yadav in *Culture of Corruption in India*, to build integrity, we need to improve service delivery by focusing on public sector accountability, we must safeguard the rule of law and promote governmental accountability and transparency, and we must build our anti-corruption capacity all across society—in Parliament, watchdog and enforcement agencies, the judiciary, and civil society.[4]

Lack of accountability by civil servants is a central issue. And South Africa is fortunate in that we already have in place most of the pillars that support transparency and accountability: the Constitution, the rule of law, the public prosecutor, and a free press. But we are in the unfortunate position of having these institutions eroded by government intervention. It will be doubly difficult for us to recover these institutions if they are abused and torn down. Each of these structures depends on the others, and stress on one of them intensifies pressure on the others; when several of these structures are diminished, the system can no longer support sustainable democratic development, and collapse becomes inevitable. It is imperative that we protect these remaining institutions if we are to save our country from becoming yet another failing African nation.

To build integrity we must also include it in economic reform, provide expert assistance on integrity-related issues, create partnerships between government and civil institutions to disseminate information, and raise public awareness through the media, NGOs, and South African citizens. A strategy of integrity should result in a broad range of reforms with the objective of creating systemic change, improved public-service delivery, and an enabling environment for developing the private sector.

Ideally, political leadership would have the political vision to execute these reforms. But in the absence of official leadership, it is encumbent on all of us ordinary South Africans to use our power and influence to drive the process of achieving reform and creating a nation of peace and prosperity. We know what needs to change, and we can devise solutions tailored to our needs. We simply cannot rely on the government to build integrity. Government efforts fail when citizen support and confidence are absent.

This is more than evident in the Gauteng e-Toll system. The ANC has tried repeatedly to force Gauteng road users to pay tolls on the oversubscribed national highways, but motorists have refused to be duped into paying for a system that we regard as unnecessary, that we believe our taxes should have paid for, and especially after we got a whiff of an international company earning the management rights. The government has resorted to a broad range of tactics to enforce subscription to the e-Toll system, from having metropolitan police departments intimidate motorists to threatening non-renewal of car licences for vehicles with unpaid e-Toll accounts. The public has formed a united force to take the government to court to delay implementation. The fight continues.

To launch a programme of integrity and build it into our democracy, we need as many stakeholders as possible—ordinary citizens, activists, and high-profile opinion makers. Committed South Africans should tackle one area of concern at a time and then link them together. We don't need any remarkable talent to participate. All we need to do is put the common welfare ahead of our particular interests, act honestly in every aspect of our lives, and sensitise our compatriots at every opportunity to the devastating effects of corruption on the development of our country. We can stop tolerating substandard service delivery. When a cohesive group comprising all sectors of the populace says, 'No more!', the government has to take the fight against corruption seriously.

No subgroup of South Africans is superior to another. We are equal. We are all entitled to live in a prosperous country, where we can work at jobs of our choice earning wages of our own determination, where we can send our children to school confident that they are receiving a sound education, where we can go jogging in the neighbourhoods without carrying a can of mace or taking a guard dog along—and where investors are willing to invest because they're confident that their assets are protected by the law. This is surely possible if we all unite to demand the kind of future that majority rule promises. Let us all be accountable and strive for that future.

NOTES

FOREWORD

1. See, for example: Jones, G & J George, (2015) *Essentials of Contemporary Management*, sixth edition, McGraw Hill Education, p. 340
2. Grossman, V (1997) *Forever Flowing*, Northwestern University Press, Illinois
3. South African Communist Party, O'Malley Archives, Nelson Mandela Foundation. https://www.nelsonmandela.org/omalley/cis/omalley/OMalleyWeb/03lv02424/04lv02730/05lv03188/06lv03217.htm
4. Williams, WE (2014) Africa: A tragic continent, 19 October 2014, Townhall.com

CHAPTER 3. CONSIDERING SOCIALISM

1. http://www.dailymaverick.co.za/article/2013-07-11-the-tripartite-alliance-is-an-anachronism/
2. http://www.telegraph.co.uk/news/worldnews/africaandindianocean/southafrica/9728147/Analysis-Jacob-Zuma-has-some-achievements-but-needs-a-vision-for-the-future.html
3. http://www.polity.org.za/article/sa-kgalema-motlanthe-address-by-the-deputy-president-of-south-africa-during-the-24th-congress-of-the-socialist-international-cape-town-international-convention-centre-cape-town-30082012-2012-08-30
4. http://www.dailymaverick.co.za/article/2014-10-16-africa-check-does-sa-really-employ-more-civil-servants-than-the-us/#.VNkREVWUf3p
5. Breytenbach, Adele, and Jannie Rossouw (2013) An analysis of remuneration trends in the South African civil service, 2005 to

2012, *Tydskr.vir Geesteswet.* (online) 53 (4), pp. 635–50

6. http://businesstech.co.za/news/general/74650/
former-eskom-ceo-paid-far-more-than-thought/

7. http://www.newstatesman.com/politics/2014/01/
south-africas-emerging-new-left-birth-new-socialist-party

8. http://www.economist.com/news/special-report/21570840-nordic-
countries-are-reinventing-their-model-capitalism-says-adrian

9. As above

10. Mashaba, H (2012) Global crisis has socialist roots, so try capitalism,
Business Report 4 (September)

11. http://www.moneyweb.co.za/moneyweb-economic-trends/
sa-capitalist-nation

12. As above

13. As above

14. As above

15. As above

16. As above

17. South African Government (2014) Twenty Year Review, http://www.
thepresidency-dpme.gov.za/news/Documents/20%20Year%20Review.pdf

CHAPTER 4. PAYING FOR THE SAFETY NET

1. http://beta2.statssa.gov.za/publications/Report-03-10-06/Report-03-10-
06March2014.pdf

2. http://www.nda.org.za/docs/Research%20Report%20-%20State%20
of%20poverty%20in%209%20provinces%20of%20SA.PDF

3. Emphasis added

4. http://www.thepresidency-dpme.gov.za/news/Documents/20%20
Year%20Review.pdf

5. http://www.sassa.gov.za/index.php/knowledge-centre/
statistical-reports?download=355:statistical-report-10-of-2014

6. http://www.southafrica.info/business/economy/policies/budget2014h.
htm

7. Emphasis added

8. http://www.sahistory.org.za/article/
south-africa%E2%80%99s-key-economic-policies-changes-1994-2013

9. http://beta2.statssa.gov.za/publications/Report-03-10-06/Report-03-10-
06March2014.pdf

CHAPTER 5. JOBS, RIGHTS AND LAWS

1. http://www.labour.gov.za/DOL/about-us
2. http://www.thepresidency-dpme.gov.za/news/Documents/20%20 Year%20Review.pdf
3. http://mg.co.za/article/2014-07-29-sas-unemployment-rate-spirals-further-into-the-record-books
4. http://acceleratecapetown.co.za/agm-2014-herman-mashaba-current-government-policies-happy-started-business-apartheid/
5. http://mg.co.za/article/2014-05-05-employment-down-for-first-quarter-of-2014
6. http://www.engineeringnews.co.za/article/growing-youth-unemployment-requires-urgent-attention-in-the-run-up-to-workers-day-2015-04-29/article_comments:1
7. As above
8. As above
9. http://mg.co.za/article/2014-05-05-employment-down-for-first-quarter-of-2014
10. http://edition.cnn.com/2011/WORLD/africa/01/16/tunisia.fruit.seller.Bouazizi
11. http://www.thepresidency-pme.gov.za/news/Documents/20%20 Year%20Review.pdf
12. http://www.bdlive.co.za/articles/2011/12/12/loane-sharp-restrictive-labour-laws-in-need-of-a-rethink;jsessionid=D9D132735ECA47621E039D32E5DBBD5F.present2.bdfm
13. http://constitutionallyspeaking.co.za/bill-of-rights/
14. http://www.chr.up.ac.za/chr_old/centre_publications/constitlaw/pdf/39-Freedom%20and%20Security.pdf
15. http://finweek.com/2013/10/24/corporate-news-report-highlights-factors-that-challenge-south-african-smes/
16. As above
17. http://english.caixin.com/2011-12-30/100344583.html
18. http://businesstech.co.za/news/international/70455/south-africa-sinks-in-economic-freedom-ranking/
19. http://mg.co.za/article/2012-08-06-ilo-sa-labour-laws-arent-fuelling-unemployment
20. http://www.tradingeconomics.com/south-africa/unemployment-rate
21. http://thenewage.co.za/blogdetail.aspx?mid=186&blog_id=2914
22. As above
23. http://www.labour.gov.za/DOL/about-us

CHAPTER 6. DISCONTENT AND PROTESTS

1. http://www.thoughtleader.co.za/chrisrodrigues/2010/04/05/on-revolutionary-songs/
2. http://www.gov.za/documents/constitution/chapter-2-bill-rights#17
3. http://www.r2k.org.za/wp-content/uploads/gatheringsGuide_WEB.pdf
4. As above
5. http://www.iol.co.za/pretoria-news/opinion/our-protest-culture-is-far-from-dead-1.1645081#.Uzt8CvmSzY6
6. http://www.newstatesman.com/blogs/world-affairs/2012/08/behind-marikana-massacre
7. http://www.brainyquote.com/quotes/quotes/b/bayardrust109490.html
8. http://www.aljazeera.com/indepth/features/2014/03/south-africa-wave-discontentment-2014312131838235849.html
9. As above
10. http://www.timeslive.co.za/politics/2011/04/18/ficksburg-mayor-scoffs-at-towns-water-shortage
11. http://www.iol.co.za/pretoria-news/opinion/our-protest-culture-is-far-from-dead-1.1645081#.Uzt8CvmSzY6
12. Professor Peter Alexander holds the Research Chair in Social Change at the University of Johannesburg
13. http://mg.co.za/article/2012-04-13-a-massive-rebellion-of-the-poor
14. http://www.sahistory.org.za/article/south-africa%E2%80%99s-key-economic-policies-changes-1994-2013
15. Kongwa, KS (2012) An investigation of the persistence of rural poverty in South Africa: The case of the OR Tambo District Municipality, PhD thesis, Fort Hare University, https://www.google.co.za/url?sa=t&rct=j&q=&esrc=s&source=web&cd=1&cad=rja&uact=8&ved=0CBwQFjAAahUKEwjGiJDku5bGAh-VDjNsKHVB-AMA&url=http%3A%2F%2Fcontentpro.seals.ac.za%2Fiii%2Fcpro%2Fapp%3Fid%3D0270251163277782%26item-Id%3D1007577%26lang%3Deng%26service%3Dblob%26suite%3D-def&ei=1ESBVcbOIMOY7gbQ_IGADA&usg=AFQjCNGXBrhWrlIldZcu-fU04YNlwFvlK_A&bvm=bv.96041959,d.ZGU
16. http://www.lowcosthousingsouthafrica.co.za/rdp_homes_south_africa.html
17. Besada, H (2007) Fragile stability: Post-apartheid South Africa, Working Paper no. 27, Centre for International Governance Innovation, https://www.google.co.za/1?sa=t&rct=j&q=&esrc=s&source=web&cd=6&cad=rja&uact=8&ved=0CDUQFjAFahUKEwiMq8favZ

bGAhUomtsKHTPiALY&url=http%3A%2F%2Fmercury.z.2Fserv
iceengine%2FFiles%2FISN%2F39546%2Fipublicationdocument_
singledocument%2F0560560c-67b4-44b8-a05b-
54f968f76008%2Fen%2FWP_27.pdf&ei=2UaBVczaFKi07gazxIOwCw&u
sg=AFQjCNEPFrw-tymqdUrUYIPRAS5lhu4Svg&bvm=bv.96041959,d.
ZGU

18. Fedderke, J (undated) A case of polarization paralysis: The debate
    surrounding a growth strategy for South Africa, Department of
    Economics, University of the Witwatersrand, https://www.google.co.za/
    l?sa=t&rct=j&q=&esrc=s&source=web&cd=1&cad=rja&uact=8&ved=0C
    B4QFjAAahUKEwiGxvDKv5bGAhXDF9sKHZYCAKM&url=http%3A%
    2F%2Fwww.econrsa.org%2Fsystem%2Ffiles%2Fpublications%2Fpolicy_
    papers_interest%2Fpp01_interest.pdf&ei=0UiBVcaZFMO
    v7AaWhYCYCg&usg=AFQjCNHcMtmEnGt6-QrpZX9_
    KXpTK1zGFQ&bvm=bv.96041959,d.ZGU

19. http://www.thepresidency-pme.gov.za/news/Documents/20%20
    Year%20Review.pdf

20. http://www.pmg.org.za/docs/2005/050216booklets.htm

21. http://www.trademarksa.org/news/sas-trade-and-investment-1994-2014

22. http://www.tradingeconomics.com/south-africa/balance-of-trade

23. http://www.tradingeconomics.com/south-africa/agriculture-value-
    added-percent-of-gdp-wb-data.html

24. http://www.sahistory.org.za/article/public-protest-democratic-south-africa

25. http://www.powermanium.com/public/davies62.pdf

26. http://mg.co.za/data/2014-04-28-taking-to-the-streets-who-is-protesting-
    and-why

27. http://www.powermanium.com/public/davies62.pdf

28. Marx, K and D McLennan (2000) *Karl Marx: Selected Writing*, Oxford
    University Press, Oxford, p. 284

CHAPTER 7. CORRUPTION AND CIVIC RESPONSIBILITY

1. http://c.ymcdn.com/sites/www.iodsa.co.za/resource/
   collection/2477EA3B-957A-43AC-BD29-E7C045B41AE9/IoDSA_
   Integrated_Report_2011.pdf

2. http://www.freemarketfoundation.com/about/who-we-are

3. Popper, K (2006) *The Open Society and Its Enemies*, Vol. 2, 1945, reprint
   Routledge Classics, London, p. 189

4. As above, p. 173

5. http://www.ifaisa.org/The_state_of_the_Rule_of_Law_in_South_Africa.
   html

6. http://www.dailymaverick.co.za/article/2013-12-05-analysis-perceptions-and-reality-of-corruption-in-south-africa/
7. As above
8. As above
9. As above
10. http://www.spiegel.de/international/world/corruption-violence-and-divisions-tears-at-anc-of-south-africa-a-852365.html
11. http://www.dailymaverick.co.za/article/2012-08-03-cadre-deployment-cronyism-and-the-paving-of-sas-highway-to-hell/
12. As above
13. http://www.realclearpolicy.com/articles/2012/07/27/the_growing_dangers_of_cronyism_232.html
14. http://econlib.org/library/Columns/y2012/Hendersonpropertyrights.html

CHAPTER 8. LABOUR LAWS ARE KEY

1. http://www.acts.co.za/labour-relations-act-1995/; emphasis added
2. https://www.imf.org/external/pubs/ft/scr/2005/cr05345.pdf
3. http://us-cdn.creamermedia.co.za/assets/articles/attachments/54484_final-manpower-workersday.pdf
4. http://www.indexmundi.com/g/r.aspx?v=2229
5. The rate of 26% was for the first quarter of 2015; http://www.tradingeconomics.com/south-africa/unemployment-rate
6. Kane Berman, J (2013) Bargaining councils violate both democracy and basic rights, *Business Day,* 14 October, http://irr.org.za/reports-and-publications/articles-authored-by-the-institute/bargaining-councils-violate-both-democracy-and-basic-rights-business-day-14-october-2013
7. http://www.sap.com/bin/sapcom/en_us/downloadasset.2014-08-aug-08-16.how-successful-smes-are-reinventing-global-business-pdf.html
8. http://blogs.hbr.org/2013/02/the-rise-of-the-nano-multinati/
9. http://www.sap.com/bin/sapcom/en_us/downloadasset.2014-08-aug-08-16.how-successful-smes-are-reinventing-global-business-pdf.html
10. As above
11. http://blogs.hbr.org/2013/02/the-rise-of-the-nano-multinati/
12. As above
13. http://www.academicjournals.org/article/article1380715803_Olawale%20and%20Garwe.pdf
14. Kane Berman, Bargaining councils, note 6 above
15. http://www.iol.co.za/business/companies/

woolworths-chairman-calls-for-a-new-economic-growth-philosophy-
for-sa-1.1588364

16. Kane Berman, Bargaining councils, note 6 above

CHAPTER 9. UNIONS IN A FREE ECONOMY

1. http://constitutionallyspeaking.co.za/the-free-market-foundations-
quixotic-venture/
2. http://mg.co.za/article/2013-03-08-00-bargaining-extension-fought-on-
constitutional-grounds-1
3. www.ilo.org/wcmsp5/groups/public/---ed_dialogue/---dialogue/
documents/publication/wcms_175009.pdf
4. http://www.sactwu.org.za/pr-and-news/290-sactwu-takes-note-of-free-
market-foundation-challenging-labour-law
5. As above
6. http://www.gilesfiles.co.za/common-law-2/philosophy-politics-
economics/free-market-liberalism-advocates-unbiased-labour-laws/
7. As above
8. http://www.nytimes.com/1987/08/16/weekinreview/miners-strike-in-
south-africa-raises-the-spirit-of-resistance.html?pagewanted=all&src=pm
9. http://www.dailymaverick.co.za/opinionista/2012-10-12-marikana-
prequel-num-and-the-murders-that-started-it-all
10. As above
11. As above
12. http://www.politicsweb.co.za/politicsweb/view/politicsweb/en/
page71619?oid=318905&sn=Detail&pid=71616
13. http://www.biznews.com/video/2013/10/gerhard-papenfuss/
14. http://mg.co.za/article/2014-10-14-platinum-mines-push-
for-mechanisation/
15. As above
16. As above

CHAPTER 10. AN OPEN OPPORTUNITY SOCIETY

1. http://www.da.org.za/why-the-da/vision/
2. http://www.news24.com/elections/results
3. See Principles, http://www.da.org.za/why-the-da/vision/
4. http://www.da.org.za/why-the-da/policies/job-business/
economic-policy/
5. http://www.da.org.za/why-the-da/policies/government/
governance-policy/

6. http://africacheck.org/factsheets/factsheet-south-africas-official-crime-statistics-for-201314/
7. http://beta2.statssa.gov.za/publications/P0341/P03412013.pdf
8. http://www.da.org.za/why-the-da/policies/land/land-reform-policy/
9. As above

CHAPTER 11. GETTING EDUCATION RIGHT

1. http://www.politicsweb.co.za/news-and-analysis/education-in-sa-is-verwoerd-to-blame
2. http://www.treasury.gov.za/documents/national%20budget/2015/ene/FullENE.pdf
3. As above
4. http://www.treasury.gov.za/documents/national%20budget/2015/guides/2015%20People's%20Guide%20-%20English.pdf
5. As above
6. http://www.ai.org.za/wp-content/uploads/downloads/2012/03/No.-72.The-Failing-Standard-of-Basic-Education-in-South-Africa1.pdf
7. http://www.timeslive.co.za/ilive/2015/01/06/state-education-in-south-africa---suffer-the-children-ilive
8. http://www.ai.org.za/wp-content/uploads/downloads/2012/03/No.-72.The-Failing-Standard-of-Basic-Education-in-South-Africa1.pdf
9. http://africacheck.org/reports/is-sas-education-system-the-worst-in-africa-not-according-to-the-data/
10. http://www.bdlive.co.za/national/education/2013/09/26/state-of-sas-education-a-concern
11. http://www.savethechildren.org.za/article/poor-quality-education-trapping-children-poverty
12. http://www.thepresidency-pme.gov.za/news/Documents/20%20Year%20Review.pdf
13. http://www.cepd.org.za/files/pictures/CEPD_SolomonMahlangu Lecture1_Badat_2007.pdf

CHAPTER 12. HOW CITIZENS BUILD A NATION

1. This chapter is based on a speech delivered by me at a Democratic Alliance event in May 2015
2. James Joyce, https://www.google.co.za/l?sa=t&rct=j&q=&esrc=s&source=web&cd=1&cad=rja&uact=8&ved=0CB0QFjAA&url=http%3A%2F%2Fwww.brainyquote.com%2Fquotes%2Fquotes%2Fj%2Fjamesjoyce379290.html&ei=ycCGVYGBM6iy7Qbw4YHADQ&usg=AFQjCNFYCeeq_KsEirX6DgtayQ5rFrxaLA&bvm=bv.96339352,d.ZGU

3. Jimmy Carter, speech, 14 October 1976, New York, 'Jimmy Carter Quotes,' Quotes.net, STANDS4 LLC, 2015, http://www.quotes.net/quote/54974

4. Kofi Anan, Secretary-General Address to World Summit, 14 September 2005, New York, http://www.un.org/webcast/summit2005/statements/sg.htm

CHAPTER 14. TRANSPARENCY SUSTAINS DEMOCRACY

1. http://www.news24.com/elections/news/7-of-the-worst-anc-quotes-20140326

2. South Africa PDF, http://info.worldbank.org/governance/wgi/index.aspx#countryReports

3. http://www.imf.org/external/pubs/ft/issues6/

4. Yadav, S (2014) *Culture of Corruption in India*, Orient Waterman, http://www.lulu.com/shop/satishchander-yadav/culture-of-corruption-in-india/paperback/product-21609800.html

REFERENCES

Breytenbach, Adele and Jannie Rossouw (2013), An analysis of remuneration
    trends in the South African civil service, 2005 to 2012, *Tydskr. Geesteswet*
    (online) 53 (4), pp 635–50, ISSN 0041-4751

Kane Berman, J (2013) Bargaining councils violate both democracy and
    basic rights, *Business Day*, 14 October, http://irr.org.za/reports-and-
    publications/articles-authored-by-the-institute/bargaining-councils-
    violate-both-democracy-and-basic-rights-business-day-14-october-2013

Marx, K and D McLennan (2000) *Karl Marx: Selected Writings*, Oxford
    University Press, Oxford

Mashaba, H (2012) Global crisis has socialist roots, so try capitalism, *Business
    Report* 4 (September)

Popper, K (2006) *The Open Society and Its Enemies*, Vol. 2, 1945, reprint
    Routledge Classics, London

South African Government (2014) Twenty Year Review, http://www.
    thepresidency-dpme.gov.za/news/Documents/20%20Year%20Review.
    pdf

REFERENCES